Creating Schools That Work for All of Us

A Guide to Empowered Stewardship

Benjie Howard

Patricia McDonald

Gary R. Howard

With Contributions from Wade Antonio Colwell

MIMI & TODD
PRESS

Copyrighted Material
Creating Schools That Work for All of Us: A Guide to Empowered Stewardship
Copyright © 2025 by Benjie Howard, Patricia McDonald, and Gary Howard
All Rights Reserved.
No part of this publication may be reproduced, stored in a retrieval system or transmitted, in any form or by any means—electronic, mechanical, photocopy, recording, or otherwise—without prior written permission from the publisher, except for the inclusion of brief quotations in a review.

For more information about this title or to order other books and/or electronic media, contact the publisher:
Mimi and Todd Press
1090 North Palm Canyon Drive
Suite B
Palm Springs, CA 92262
www.mimitoddpress.com

ISBN: 978-1-950089-24-6

Printed in the United States of America
Program Director: Paul J. Bloomberg
Publishing Manager: Tony Francoeur
Executive Director of Publishing: Isaac Wells
Development Editor: Dan Alpert
Copy Editor: Terri Lee Paulsen
Layout: Darlene Swanson
Cover Design: Alison Cox
Indexer: Vennesa Reid
Office Manager: Leah Tierney

Contents

Foreword vi

About the Authors viii

Welcome to Empowered Stewardship ix

Centering Community Wisdom: Honoring the Voices That Transform Schools x

Navigating the Guidebook xi

Section 1: Laying the Foundation for Empowered Stewardship 1

   Part 1: An Introduction to Empowered Stewardship and YES 2

      Transforming Schools Through Youth Empowered Stewardship 2

      The YES Origin Story 4

      What Is Stewardship? 5

   Part 2: Engaging in the Work of Empowered Stewardship 7

      Affirmation Before Reformation 8

      Empowered Stewardship Outcomes 9

   Part 3: Building Foundational Understanding for Empowered Stewardship 12

      Understanding the Achievement Triangle 12

      An Introduction to the Seven Stewardship Commitments 14

      Layers of Engagement: A Note to Leaders 15

      The Four A's 18

   Part 4: Engaging in Collaborative Inquiry 19

      The YES Collaborative Inquiry Process 20

      The YES Collaborative Inquiry Process in Practice 24

      The Five Streams of Engagement. 30

Section 2: Exploring the Streams of Engagement 33

Stream 1: The Riverbed 35

- Overview of Engagement Strategies 36
- The Achievement Triangle 39
- Questions to Consider 42
- Climate Assessment 44
- School Outcomes Assessment 47
- Stages of Organizational Growth 50
- Catalysts for Growth 54
- Kudos and Challenges 57
- The Four As 60

Stream 2: Story, Trust, & Community Journey 64

- Overview of Engagement Strategies 65
- Homelands Conversation 68
- Definition of Stewardship 72
- In Lak'ech 75
- What Is Culture? 79
- Definition of Cultural Competence 85
- ¿Quiénes Somos? (Who Are We?) 88
- Lenses of Difference 91
- Identity Triangle 94
- Culture Toss 98
- Stereotype Threat Research 102
- Stages of Personal Growth Toward Cultural Competence 105
- Personal Growth Project 111
- In My One Beat 115

Stream 3: Social Dominance to Justice for All 120

- Overview of Engagement Strategies 122
- We, the People / *Nican Tlaca* 125
- Dominance to Justice Word Association 128
- Dynamics of Social Dominance 131
- Privilege and Power Assessment 133
- Justice in the Words of Elders 137
- In My One Beat – Struggle 142

Stream 4: Intergenerational Partnership & Practice 145
- Overview of Engagement Strategies 148
- Introducing the Seven Commitments of Stewardship Practice 150
- Invitation Into the House of Learning 151
- Seven Commitments Application: Growing Classroom Practice, Classroom Culture 156
- Seven Commitments Study Groups 161
- Seven Commitments Assessment 165
- Learning From and With Colleagues 168
- Glow and Grow: Student Reflections on Teacher Practice 170
- Seven Commitments Action Research Project 179
- Seven Commitments Student-Centered Project 183

Stream 5: Creative Resistance 187
- Our Roots of Stewardship: Part 1 192
- Our Roots of Stewardship: Part 2 197
- Creative Resistance – Interpersonal 199
- Creative Resistance – Systemic 205
- Shifting the Emotional Paradigm 208
- The Desert Monsoon Model: Closing the Gap Between Student Voice and Student Agency 213
- The Desert Monsoon Model 215
- The Five Aspects of a Desert Monsoon 218

The Rainbow: A Note for Stewards 223

In Closing 224

Glossary 226

Appendices 230
- Appendix A: YES Collaborative Inquiry Template 230
- Appendix B: YES Collaborative Inquiry Snapshots 230
- Appendix C: Recommended Engagement Strategies for Each Phase of Inquiry 230

Acknowledgements 231

References 233

Index 238

Foreword

by Gary Howard

I BEGAN MY WORK IN education some 50 years ago and was fortunate enough at that time to find myself connected to a community of brilliant minds and caring hearts who were engaged in birthing the ethnic studies and multicultural education movements. These educators were passionately involved in imagining schools that could better serve all of us across our many diverse attributes—schools that could help us manifest that "beloved community" that Dr. Martin Luther King, Jr. so often invoked. Among these educators were James Banks, Carl Grant, Sonia Nieto, Geneva Gay, Christine Sleeter, and many others. Each of them, in their own way, inspired me and helped me in my efforts to formulate an approach to professional development and curriculum design that has, for the past five decades, been implemented across the country and overseas. Any degree of authenticity and effectiveness I may have achieved as an educator has come from my immersion in this community of creative and visionary educators who welcomed me to the work and continue to inspire me today.

And now, I am excited to welcome you to an expanding community of inspired educators and introduce you to an emerging approach to transformational education, Empowered Stewardship, presented here in this Guidebook. Coming at a time when there is so much need to reinvigorate and reinspire ourselves, our colleagues, our students, and our communities with a vision of the possible, a vision of what education could be, the Empowered Stewardship work is about reimagining and creating schools that work better for all of us. This process of renewal is critical precisely because there is so much pressure at this time to narrow the scope of learning, to ban books, outlaw the teaching of multiple perspectives in history and literature, and curtail much-needed conversations about race, gender identity, sexual orientation, religious diversity, and the real issues that impact our students' lives. Early in the multicultural education movement, James Banks articulated three central goals of quality education: to know, to care, and to act. These three learning intentions are at the heart of Empowered Stewardship: to know and honor our individual and collective stories, to care about the nurturing and healing of our communities, and to take action for the health and well-being of ourselves, our students, and our planet.

The team of educators engaged in developing the Empowered Stewardship approach are one, two, and even three generations younger than those of us who birthed the early movements in the 1960s and '70s. Together, they have choreographed a multigenerational dance of professional development, youth empowerment, and community engagement that truly transcends anything I could have imagined in my career. They have endowed the work with music and poetry, colorful visual imagery, movement, and evocative metaphors that inspire and enliven the minds, hearts, and bodies of students and adults alike. The Empowered Stewardship work brings creative artistry and powerful grace to the work of belonging, equity, and excellence. I trust you will find it a breath of fresh air amidst all the critical work you are already doing.

About the Authors

Benjie Howard

Benjie Howard is an author, poet, musician, wilderness guide, and educator. He is the Founder of New Wilderness Project, a wilderness-based youth education program focused on stewardship for natural and cultural communities, and the co-founder of Youth Empowered Stewardship, offering intergenerational learning opportunities in schools across the country. He is the co-author of Youth Equity Stewardship, Corwin Press, 2018, and Separation Point - The Edge of Wildness, Laguna Wilderness Press, 2021. He lives with his family in the Pacific Northwest.

Patricia McDonald

Patricia "Tmac" McDonald is a teacher, consultant, and cultural competency trainer committed to dismantling the barriers in traditional education. She has spent the last three decades helping create pathways into teaching for students underrepresented in the profession. Currently, her scholarship focuses on how authentic and responsive classroom relationships require educators to actively examine their identity, engage with discomfort, and commit to ongoing personal growth necessary to connect meaningfully with students. She and her partner split their time between a tiny house in Washington State and Mexico.

Gary Howard.

For five decades, Gary has supported educators in their efforts to create schools that work for all of us. He is the founder of the REACH Center for Multicultural Education. The author of We Can't Teach What We Don't Know: White Teachers/Multiracial Schools (3rd ed.), Teachers College Press, 2016, and We Can't Lead Where We Won't Go: An Educator's Guide to Equity, Corwin Press, 2014. He lives in the Pacific Northwest on an island in the Salish Sea.

Welcome to Empowered Stewardship

An Invitation from Benjie Howard

Welcome to the Stewardship learning journey! This guidebook is a part of a larger set of resources designed to support creative collaboration among teachers, leaders, staff, students, and families in our collective efforts to make school work better for all of us.

This specific resource is for educational professionals. It is designed to be used as your personal learning journal. It includes an overview of the Stewardship conceptual framework, learning goals, engagement strategies, and opportunities for creative expression and reflection. It should, if facilitated with care, humility, and clarity, support your growth as a person and as an educator. And when you and your colleagues approach this work with intentionality and openness, it will support your larger efforts to create schools that better serve all of your students. This guidebook is designed in alignment with a companion book, *Youth Empowered Stewardship: A Guide for Intergenerational Partnership*, which specifically engages young people as active partners in transforming schools. You will notice the use of the term Youth Empowered Stewardship (YES) and the term Empowered Stewardship throughout this guidebook.

At the same time, it should also build on and honor the good work you are already doing and inspire you with new possibilities. It should remind you of why you chose this sacred profession and why you stay in the game by reigniting your passion for the work. In the process, you can begin to re-imagine what you want for yourself and your colleagues—and what you envision together for your students, both now and in our shared future.

Note: The name Youth Empowered Stewardship and the acronym YES are used to describe the overall approach including professional learning, youth and community engagement, and more. Though all of this work is centered on student experience and outcomes, the term Empowered Stewardship is used when directly referencing professional learning with adults.

Centering Community Wisdom: Honoring the Voices That Transform Schools

An Invitation from Patricia McDonald

Decades of work in schools across the country reveal a consistent truth: the knowledge most vital for transforming educational environments is often already present within the school community. However, research shows that the voices and experiences of educators and students of color are frequently marginalized in professional learning and equity conversations, perpetuating systemic inequities and hindering meaningful progress toward just and inclusive learning environments (Delpit, 2006; Howard & Rodriguez, 2000; Milner, 2020; Paris & Alim, 2017).

Scholars emphasize that genuine school transformation begins by centering the wisdom of those most impacted by inequitable systems, particularly students and educators from marginalized communities (Gay, 2018; Ladson-Billings, 2009). As Geneva Gay (2018) states, "Culturally responsive teaching is most effective when it grows from real, reciprocal relationships with students, where their cultural knowledge, experiences, and perspectives are treated as vital assets, not deficits" (p. 45). Yet despite research showing that educators with shared cultural backgrounds are often most effective at building trust and fostering learning, these practitioners are frequently excluded from leadership and decision-making roles while change efforts remain driven by those with institutional power and privilege (Acosta & Mir, 2012; Gooden & Dantley, 2012; Khalifa et al., 2016; Villegas & Lucas, 2002).

Systemic transformation requires more than listening—it demands sustained reflection, critical self-examination, and a willingness to act on insights from historically unheard voices (Freire, 2000; hooks, 1994; Singleton, 2021; Weinstein et al., 2004). Teams engaging in the Empowered Stewardship process must be intentional about who is at the table, ensuring that diverse voices, particularly those of educators and students from marginalized communities, are positioned as co-leaders rather than tokens in school change efforts (Bertrand & Rodela, 2018; Ishimaru, 2020; Warren et al., 2009; Welton et al., 2018). When schools commit to genuine partnership structures where historically excluded voices drive vision and strategy, they unlock the possibility for authentic, lasting, and joyful transformation (Brown, 2018; Love, 2019).

Navigating the Guidebook

Creating Schools That Work for All of Us: A Guide to Empowered Stewardship is more than a book; it is an invitation to think, feel, and act differently in service to professional and organizational growth. It is a companion for individuals and teams committed to building schools where we all thrive with dignity, agency, and belonging.

Foundational Structures

The *Achievement Triangle* and the *Seven Stewardship Commitments*, both of which you will read about in Part 3, provide key foundational structures for this work. The Achievement Triangle frames the inner work required to know ourselves, our students, and our practice, while the Seven Commitments define the relational and professional habits needed to build inclusive, equitable, justice-centered learning environments. Together, they function as a throughline guiding every engagement strategy and inquiry cycle with a balance of personal/professional growth and collective responsibility.

Organization of the Guidebook

Section 1: Laying the Foundation for Empowered Stewardship

Parts 1-4 are an introduction to the key concepts you will use throughout the Empowered Stewardship process.

- **Part 1: An Introduction to Empowered Stewardship and YES** Introduces the concept of YES, shares the Origin Story, and describes the overall approach.

- **Part 2: Engaging in the Work of Empowered Stewardship** Situates the guidebook within a broader ecosystem of supports, affirming educators and outlining outcomes for cultivating schools where everyone thrives.

- **Part 3: Building Foundational Understanding for Empowered Stewardship** Provides a shared understanding of the Seven Stewardship Commitments and the Layers of Engagement that guide transformative change.

Part 4: Engaging in Collaborative Inquiry
Presents the YES Collaborative Inquiry model, integrating liberatory design and the Five Streams of Engagement to drive equity-centered action.

Section 2: Exploring the 5 Streams of Engagement

The guidebook continues with an exploration of the 5 Streams of Engagement. These Streams present practical engagement strategies organized in two ways: by Collaborative Inquiry and by the Layers of Engagement—personal, professional, and organizational. Each strategy includes clear, detailed guidance for implementation, tailored to its specific purpose and context.

- **Stream 1 – The Riverbed:** Establishes the relational and strategic foundations needed to support equity work through data-informed inquiry and collective alignment.
- **Stream 2 – Story, Trust, and Community Journey:** Uses storytelling to deepen trust, affirm identity, and build authentic community across difference.
- **Stream 3 – Social Dominance to Justice for All:** Confronts historical and systemic inequities by shifting from social dominance to shared power and justice for all.
- **Stream 4 – Intergenerational Partnership & Practice:** Applies the Seven Commitments to classroom and leadership practice through action research and professional collaboration.
- **Stream 5 – Creative Resistance:** Harnesses creative thinking, expression, and solutions to transform harm into healing through arts-based, justice-driven engagement.

Implementing the Engagement Strategies

The engagement strategies outlined in each Stream are explicitly designed to support your work within the YES Collaborative Inquiry model. A brief description at the start of each strategy provides clear, detailed guidance for implementing each strategy according to its intended purpose and context.

Each Stream begins with a conceptual overview that grounds the content in pedagogy and research, followed by a set of engagement strategies. These strategies are practical, participatory learning experiences that can be used in team meetings, professional learning, classrooms, or community gatherings.

You do not need to move through this book linearly, but we encourage you to approach each Stream with intention. Each engagement strategy includes:

- **Description** of the purpose and rationale behind the activity
- **Independent and/or Collaborative Work** designed to foster trust, build capacity, and surface diverse perspectives
- **Learning Intentions** to clarify outcomes and guide facilitation

- **Discussion and/or Reflection Prompts** organized around the Stewardship *Achievement Triangle* framework: *Know Self, Know Students, Know Practice*

Enjoy the Journey

Use this book as a learning journal, a team guide, an opportunity for practice, and a springboard for action. These supports are not designed as a solution or a rigid prescription for closing access and opportunity gaps. They are, rather, a set of catalysts—experiences, engagement strategies, and frameworks designed to draw out the wisdom already in your community and grow people from where they are. Some engagements will stir emotions, surface hard truths, or challenge long-held assumptions. That is part of the work. Stewardship requires courage, creativity, and care. Return to the engagement strategies often. Revisit your reflections. Share your insights with others. Use the tools not as one-time events but as catalysts for sustained growth.

This workbook is meant to support your role in shaping a more just and joyful school and community.

Additional downloadable tools, extended examples, videos, and printable resources are available on the Mimi & Todd Press website.

Use the QR code below to access the full library of companion materials and check back as the authors continue to share what they develop.

Section 1: Laying the Foundation for Empowered Stewardship

Transforming schools into equitable, inclusive, and vibrant communities begins with shared purpose and deep relational work. Section One lays the foundation for Empowered Stewardship, guiding readers through four parts that establish the why, what, and how of this transformative approach. Across this section, you will encounter a powerful invitation: to co-create a culture of care, creativity, and collective action rooted in the lived experiences of students, educators, and community members.

Together, Parts 1-4 outline the philosophical and practical architecture of YES: a holistic, arts-based, equity-centered approach that engages both youth and adults in reshaping school ecosystems from the inside out. The frameworks, commitments, and inquiry process presented in this section are not static or prescriptive; they are living tools designed to grow with your context, amplify the wisdom in your community, and guide courageous, collaborative work. Whether you are a teacher, leader, student, or community partner, you are invited to begin this journey not as a passive participant but as a steward, someone who leads with care, acts with knowledge, and envisions a future where every learner can thrive.

Part 1: An Introduction to Empowered Stewardship and YES

This is your introduction to Empowered Stewardship and the Youth Empowered Stewardship (YES) framework, a dynamic, arts-based, equity-centered approach that engages students, educators, families, and leaders as co-creators of school culture and systemic change.

Grounded in over four decades of research and practice, YES blends intergenerational collaboration, culturally responsive pedagogy, and student voice to build school communities where every learner thrives. In the pages ahead, you'll explore the meaning of Stewardship, the origin story of YES, and how it has evolved into an integrated approach that centers agency, belonging, and systemic transformation. These foundations prepare you for the engagement strategies that follow, and invite you to reflect on how your own school community can grow a culture of care, knowledge, and healing action.

Transforming Schools Through Youth Empowered Stewardship

Transforming schools into equitable, inclusive, and culturally sustaining communities requires more than just policy shifts—it demands authentic, intergenerational partnerships that center student voices, creative expression (the art of teaching), and shared leadership. Intergenerational partnerships transcend professional roles, across generations of learners, and the many beautiful differences that live in our educational spaces, so together we are unified in our belief that we can deepen our connections for community wellbeing. This work honors the generational contributions from communities whose ancestors have been here since time immemorial, those who were brought here by force, and those who arrived here via migration. By bridging generational divides, intergenerational partnerships foster mentorship, innovation, and a deeper understanding of diverse lived experiences.

Youth Empowered Stewardship (YES) is an arts-based, equity-focused pathway fostering lasting collaboration between students and adults through iterative, collaborative inquiry. YES engages participants in creative, reflective, and transformative experiences that position every community member as co-designers of their learning environments, actively dismantling traditional hierarchies. YES promotes empowerment as a fundamental way of being, where every voice matters, every story holds value, and every learner thrives.

Growing this culture requires both the willingness and capacity to forge authentic relationships, supported by deep self-awareness and empathy-driven practices.

Grounded in learner agency and culturally responsive practices, YES envisions schools as vibrant ecosystems where relationships and shared responsibilities work together to shape the educational experience. Building this culture means nurturing trust, honoring every voice, and ensuring that leaders, teachers, students, and families each play an active role in creating equitable and empowering learning spaces. The two dimensions below, relationships and roles and responsibilities, work in concert to sustain this vision.

Relationships: The Foundation for Shared Growth

Strong, equitable relationships form the backbone of thriving school communities. In YES, these relationships are cultivated with intention, reciprocity, and respect for every stakeholder's voice, creating conditions where:

- Empathy, trust, and sustained dialogue are intentionally nurtured to strengthen connections across the school community.
- Families participate as equal partners, sharing power and shaping school culture alongside educators and students.
- Family partnerships extend into the home, where parents and caregivers help children reflect on their learning processes, model self-awareness, and reinforce strategies for growth.
- Engagement moves beyond attendance at school-led events to authentic, two-way partnerships where families and educators learn with and from one another.
- Schools draw on Karen Mapp's Dual Capacity Framework to build the skills, confidence, and shared capacity of both educators and families to co-create equitable learning environments.
- Asset-based collaboration replaces deficit-based thinking, honoring families' cultural knowledge and lived experiences as essential to student success.

Roles and Responsibilities: Co-Creating the Learning Experience

In YES, every stakeholder plays an active role in shaping an equitable and empowering learning environment. Shared leadership, mutual accountability, and a commitment to learner agency guide how:

- Leaders create inclusive, courageous, and visionary spaces for shared decision-making, embedding equity into every aspect of organizational practice.
- Teachers act as facilitators and partners, honoring students' cultural and social identities while nurturing curiosity, creativity, and brilliance through liberatory pedagogy.
- Students serve as active agents of change, using artistic expression and lived experience to challenge inequities, inspire peers, and affirm their own identities.

- Families contribute as co-creators of school culture, participating in meaningful decision-making processes and sustained collaboration.
- Collective responsibility and creative collaboration ensure that every voice—student, family, educator, and leader—shapes the school's ongoing transformation toward equity and empowerment.

The YES Origin Story

YES is grounded in over 40 years of Gary Howard's research and work in schools across the United States, Canada, and Australia (Howard, 2014; Howard, 2016). In 2004, Maketa Born and Benjie Howard founded an arts-based, youth-centered component aligned with Gary's framework, weaving together original music, creative expression, and experiential, wilderness-based learning. For the next decade, they shared this work in school districts implementing Gary's equity process. In 2013, Wade Antonio Colwell joined the team, bringing his music, artistry, and expertise in ethnic studies and restorative practices, helping to deepen and expand the approach over the next decade. Wade and Benjie built out the youth component and published a student guide to the work in partnership with Corwin Press and Gary Howard (Colwell & Howard, 2018). Coauthor Patricia McDonald brings over 30 years of experience in educational collaboration with Gary, beginning in 1994 as staff at the REACH Center for Multicultural Education and now as a lead consultant and partner in the process of integrating both the adult professional development and youth engagement components of the YES approach. As a tenured faculty member in teacher education, her scholarship centers on cultivating educators' capacity to develop pedagogical practices that are responsive and student-centered.

Today, the work is enriched by an expanded and diverse team of educators, leaders, authors, and artists from across the United States, Mexico, and Canada. YES represents a fully integrated, intergenerational learning pathway for both youth and adults. It is rooted in the arts, experiential and Indigenous pedagogy, the long arch of research and efforts to transform schools, and the practice of *creative resistance*. The work is further strengthened by the contributions of Paul Bloomberg and Barb Pitchford's *Impact Teams* collaborative inquiry model to more comprehensively create the conditions for systemic equity. Their work on collective efficacy and learner agency deepens YES's commitment to equity-driven, student-centered learning. Together, these frameworks form a dynamic approach that ensures public education empowers more of us, across more of our differences, to succeed on our own terms, without sacrificing who we are.

Through reflective arts-based practices and student-led initiatives, YES strengthens school culture by guiding leaders, educators, and students in co-creating an intergenerational learning environment that is responsive, just, and sustaining. Research indicates that democratic education is fundamentally about instilling values such as freedom, equality, and justice within the school community (Wijaya Mulya et al., 2022). The active participation of students in decision-making and crafting school culture not only enhances their educational experience but also prepares them to be informed and engaged citizens. The YES model builds the collective capacity of schools and districts to dismantle inequities—reducing opportunity gaps, disrupting exclusionary disciplinary practices, and advancing a culture where every learner thrives with agency, creativity, and purpose. By centering arts, culture, and student voice, YES fosters deeper connections, creative problem-solving, and transformative action, ensuring that schools are not just places of learning but spaces of belonging, liberation, and joyful expression.

What Is Stewardship?

STEWARDSHIP is ACTION, rooted in KNOWLEDGE, in CARE of OURSELVES, our FAMILIES, HUMANITY, and the LAND.

At its core, Stewardship is about communities coming together to do deep, transformative work at the personal, professional, and organizational levels—work that will help us grow a culture of Stewardship across professional roles, generations of learners (adult professionals, students, and families), and the many beautiful and vital differences that live in our communities. We will explore in more depth the meaning of culture, equity, and stewardship throughout the engagement strategies outlined in Section 2 of this guidebook. For now, *culture* is the intricate and complex ecosystem of relationships, norms, traditions, and ways of being that make up who we are and how we see ourselves together as a community of people. *Equity* (in contrast to "equality") is grounded in the reality that we do not all start from the same place. In the context of schooling, it means recognizing that some students require more or different resources and supports than others and that we leverage our personal competencies and professional responsive practices to ensure that each child receives what they need to succeed in school and beyond. In order for this to happen, we also work to eliminate persistent predictive barriers to success related to race, ZIP code, and other dimensions of difference.

Therefore, Stewardship is about being responsible for and caring for something beyond ourselves. In this context, it means taking care of, serving, and being in relationships with people who are different from us and having the capacity to contribute to the good of the community. Bringing this all together, our goal in this work is to support you and your community in creating a Culture of Stewardship, which will require us to address how the school feels, how it functions, and the outcomes we produce together.

At the heart of the Stewardship work is a deep belief in the power of relationships. The phrase "relationships precede learning" was coined by three Minneapolis-area educators in the 1990s and grew out of their observation and documentation of the behaviors and beliefs of teachers who were highly effective in their work with diverse and often marginalized students (Shade et al., 1997). Much more work has been done since then, consistently confirming the connection between teachers knowing students' stories, students having relational trust in their teachers, and academic success (Emdin, 2017; Gay, 2018; Hammond, 2014; Milner, 2020; Safir & Dugan, 2021).

We have never met a successful adult who "came up hard" who cannot identify the *one* teacher, coach, or bus driver who made all the difference—that one person who knew them, saw a future for them, and inspired them to see an alternate path for themselves. The problem, however, lives in the "one who got out" story, consistent across regions and throughout generations—the one teacher who changed the trajectory for one child remains an inspirational theme, yet an extremely limited narrative arc for the systemic transformation of public education. The question for us, knowing that relationships precede learning, is how do we change the dynamic of *one* teacher to include *all* teachers and *one* student to include *all* students, not the one who got out but the many who come back or stay in the neighborhood and contribute to its uplift? How do we grow and expand a through-line of relationship among professionals, students, and families consistently and systemically? This is the question that Stewardship invites us to engage.

Just as authentic and caring relationships precede deeper engagement and higher achievement for students, improving the complex web of relationships across the many differences in your school community should precede any meaningful structural changes in policy or professional practice. Over the years, our Stewardship team has worked in many high-poverty schools doing the work to become high-performing. While the strategies used to turn a school around are as diverse as the communities they serve, there are some consistent patterns. In places where good things are happening for racially diverse, poor, and other marginalized students, the focus has been on the core elements of quality schooling; courageous and collaborative leadership; skilled, passionate, culturally competent educators; students who are challenged, engaged and affirmed, and a clear and intentional focus on the ecosystem of relationships in and around school.

In order to make fundamental structural changes in policy, curriculum, hiring, and retention, graduation rates, AP enrollment, discipline practices, and other school outcomes, we are compelled to challenge long-standing norms in the way we see ourselves and how we view the entire process and profession of schooling. We are asked to broaden the lens through which we view our work to include our history of inclusion and exclusion as a nation, to learn from those voices that have not been included, which represent the same cultural and racial groups that our schools have not equitably served. Rather than perpetuating business as usual, Stewardship calls us to imagine and grow a culture of radical inclusion, of belonging, of ever-increasing equitable practice and outcomes for students and adults.

We focus on Stewardship both as a way of being together in our schools and as a way of expanding and deepening what we consider to be educational excellence. The concept of Stewardship allows us to expand our notion of excellence beyond preparedness for college and career, and more toward preparedness for giving back and taking care, toward readiness and capacity to restore health to self, to family, to culture and community, to democracy, to humanity, and to the land. In short, this work is about growing a culture now and imagining and working toward a future rooted in care, knowledge, and healing action.

What are you thinking? What do you want to remember?

Part 2: Engaging in the Work of Empowered Stewardship

This Part introduces the broader learning ecosystem that surrounds this guidebook, including live youth engagements, professional learning for educators, leadership coaching, and community events. These supports are not fixed solutions—they are catalysts, designed to grow your team's capacity from within and to amplify the strengths already present in your community.

As you read, you'll learn how YES advances democracy through shared leadership, civic participation, and creative expression. You'll explore the principle of *affirmation before reformation*, which frames this work as an act of honoring educators and students alike. You'll also encounter a progression of *outcomes*, developed from decades of research and school partnerships, that can help you track and guide your progress toward equity, inclusion, and thriving learning environments. Part 2 invites you to imagine your school not just as a site of academic instruction, but as a living, breathing part of a democratic society that prepares all learners to lead with courage, creativity, and purpose.

Advancing Democracy

YES advances democracy by transforming schools into vibrant spaces of civic engagement, shared leadership, and collective action. By guiding leaders, educators, and students in co-creating an intergenerational learning environment that is responsive, just, and sustaining, YES nurtures the democratic values of freedom, equality, and social justice (Wijaya Mulya et al., 2022).

Democratic education thrives when students actively participate in governance, decision-making, and shaping the culture of their schools, preparing them to be informed, engaged citizens who contribute to a just society. The YES model builds the collective capacity of schools and districts to dismantle inequities by reducing opportunity gaps, disrupting exclusionary disciplinary practices, and cultivating a culture where every learner thrives with agency, creativity, and purpose.

By centering arts, culture, and student voice, YES not only fosters deeper connections and creative problem-solving but also empowers young people to exercise their civic power. Schools become not just places of learning but incubators of democracy—where belonging, liberation, and joyful expression are essential conditions for meaningful participation and transformative action.

Affirmation Before Reformation

Just as we strive to apply an assets-based lens to the children we serve, Empowered Stewardship also affirms the inherent goodness and brilliance of educators. This work is about good people doing hard work, not about bad people messing up. Too much of the politics and past rhetoric of school reform has been anti-teacher and anti-public education. As a result, teachers and school leaders are hungry for affirmation, for recognition of the difficulty and worth of their work. Many of the engagements in this guidebook are designed to create a trusting environment where educators can talk with each other, not in overly scripted and controlled ways, but in an authentic environment of mutual respect and support. This affirmational tone enhances our willingness to critically reflect on our practice, share our struggles and strengths, and be more open to reframing our beliefs and behaviors in the service of students. As Geneva Gay made clear many years ago, if we are serious about growing our people and transforming our schools, then it is critical that we put "affirmation before reformation."

This work has grown in partnership with school districts for more than five decades. It has evolved through periods of expansion and innovation, through the emergence of ethnic studies in the 1970s, the multicultural education movement in the 1980s, "diversity trainings" in the 1990s, through the challenges of the No Child Left Behind era that began in the early 2000s, and into the Diversity, Equity, and Inclusion era. Our use of arts-based approaches commenced in the 2000s, and more recently, we began to merge our equity efforts with restorative practices, social-emotional learning, identity work, and belonging. Across the decades, we have also weathered multiple attacks on our efforts to make schools work better for everyone. We are currently living through a resurgent set of assaults on queer students and families, on Black history, Indigenous history, and on people of color in general. These attacks have been uniquely damaging by framing approaches that support historically marginalized communities as "too woke," or anti-straight, anti-White, anti-Christian, and anti-American. This reemergence of Lost Cause and White Supremacist grievance narratives is taking place simultaneously with efforts from the political left that never miss an opportunity to call people out for racism and bigotry, but too often fail to do the harder work of listening to and engaging with people with whom we disagree. Together, these two phenomena compel us to lean deeper than we ever have into the affirmation of one another's humanity and dignity, to imagine ourselves and each other as part of a larger democratic project, with public education at its center. This is the terrain that Stewardship invites us to explore.

Empowered Stewardship Outcomes

The outcomes presented here represent observations and information compiled from case studies in Kentucky, Washington, and Illinois, where the youth and professional learning tracks have been in place for at least three years, some as long as 10 years. The outcomes also represent survey and achievement data from multiple partner districts across the United States over the last two decades. Time frames for the actualization of the four levels of outcomes differ depending on the size of a district, leadership commitment, level of collaboration, willingness to empower grassroots players, political factors, building-level leadership, willingness to include student and community voices, and many other factors. In the midst of these complexities, these outcomes have been consistently achieved, especially when the process and the strategies are implemented in a way that allows for local and internalized ownership of the learning journey, and where creativity and collaboration are encouraged. We have also learned that these outcomes are realized more deeply and more quickly when there is a high level of collaboration between our Stewardship team and key building and district stakeholders. It should also be stated that the work of Stewardship itself has evolved and been profoundly improved and transformed because of the creative approaches and strategies we've learned from our client partners. The work is never static, always dynamic and adaptive.

Level One Outcomes:
- Shift in the tone and depth of adult and student conversation
- More trust, more honesty, more safety, more bravery
- Willingness to take on difficult topics
- Clearer leadership focus on equity
- Families and community are invited into the learning journey

Level Two Outcomes:
- Improvement in the climate of inclusion for students
- Increased belongingness, connectedness
- Reduced incidents of bullying and harassment
- More positive student and adult relationships
- Students empowered to speak their truth
- Teachers empowered to speak their truth

Level Three Outcomes:
- Broad implementation of Stewardship practices
- The Seven Commitments of Stewardship are embedded across the system
- Critical thinking about complex socio-political topics is increased
- Curriculum and materials represent the diversity in the community
- Support staff engaged in Stewardship work
- "Leading for Equity" guides all decision-making
- Student ambassadors are included in high-level decision-making

Level Four Outcomes:
- Significant reduction in educational disparities
- Discipline and special education referrals are equitably applied
- Achievement levels increase for all students
- Access to higher-level courses increases for all
- School is centered in the life of the community
- Stewardship, belonging, and academic achievement are equally valued
- Graduation and college attendance rates increase

Small Group Conversation

- For which of these outcomes are you presently gathering data?

- For which outcomes do you have evidence showing significant progress has already been made?

- For which of these outcomes would you say there is the most need for action now?

- Are there other outcomes you would want to include?

Note: We will be revisiting these outcomes periodically throughout the Stewardship process. We encourage you and your colleagues to keep these in mind as you plan and implement your work.

What are you thinking? What do you want to remember?

Part 3: Building Foundational Understanding for Empowered Stewardship

Before we can transform schools through Empowered Stewardship, we must begin with shared understanding. Part 3 invites you to explore the core commitments and conceptual frameworks that anchor the Stewardship approach. These foundations support the mindsets and actions needed to build inclusive, equity-centered learning communities where every learner and educator can thrive.

You will begin by unpacking the *Seven Stewardship Commitments*—a set of shared aspirational values and culturally responsive practices. These Commitments clarify what it means to be a steward in a school setting and what it looks like when equity lives in our daily interactions, environments, and decisions. Next, you'll explore the *Layers of Engagement*, a framework that emphasizes how change must occur at multiple levels: personal, professional, organizational, and structural. Rather than relying on top-down mandates, Stewardship invites change from the inside out and the outside in, anchored in relational trust and systemic awareness.

You'll also be introduced to the *Four As*, Alignment, Accountability, Assessment, and Advocacy, as a reflective tool for leaders to assess progress, deepen shared ownership, and ensure that student and community voice guide the work. These ideas and frameworks will serve as critical tools throughout your Stewardship journey, helping you translate intention into sustainable action.

Understanding the Achievement Triangle

The Achievement Triangle (see Figure 1) provides a foundational framework for the YES Collaborative Inquiry process, offering a clear and actionable model for growing culturally responsive practice through three interrelated domains: knowledge of self, knowledge of students, and knowledge of practice. Rooted in Stewardship and equity, this model supports both individual and collective learning by guiding intentional reflection and action across each domain.

A culture of Stewardship requires both the will and the skill to build authentic relationships across lines of difference, as well as the commitment to know ourselves more deeply. Within YES, this reflective journey is not peripheral—it is essential. Like a three-legged stool, each side of the Achievement Triangle must be engaged to ensure balanced, sustainable, and measurable growth.

This framework will surface throughout your Stewardship journey, informing learning engagements that strengthen your self-awareness, deepen your understanding of those you serve, and sharpen your instructional and leadership practice. It can also guide your team's professional learning efforts, especially when responding to inequities or identifying student groups who are not yet being well served. As stewards of learning ecosystems, we take on the responsibility of growing in all three areas so that we can better support the growth of others.

Figure 1: The Achievement Triangle

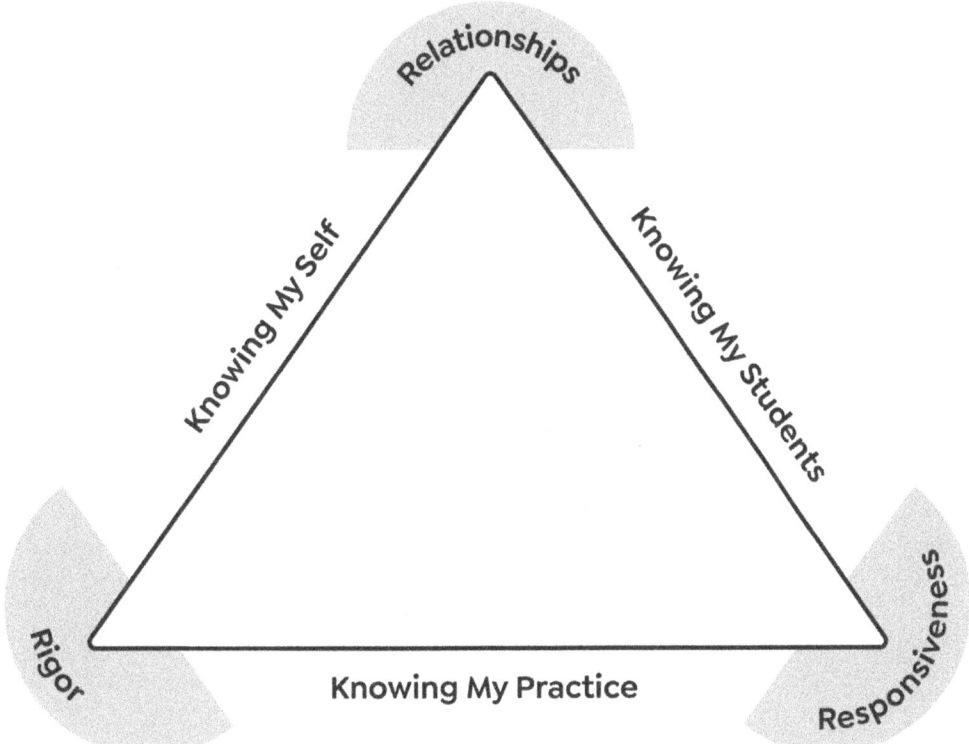

An Introduction to the Seven Stewardship Commitments

The Seven Stewardship Commitments (see Figure 2) define what it means to embody the role of a Steward within an equity-centered school ecosystem. These commitments serve as core practices for how we show up, engage with others, and create environments where every learner is seen, valued, and supported. Together, they represent a shared vision for culturally responsive practice and collective responsibility. Each commitment will be explored in greater depth in Section 2, Stream 4.

Figure 2: The Seven Commitments of Stewardship

	1. Our cultural identities are affirmed and valued
	2. Our relationships are rooted in earned respect and cultural humility
	3. Our learning environments are inviting, culturally relevant, and vibrant
	4. Our expectations and actions amplify adult and student brilliance
	5. Our interactions celebrate and adapt to diverse ways of knowing, learning, and being
	6. Our educational experiences reinforce creative and critical thinking
	7. Our interactions honor individual aspirations and collective responsibilities

Layers of Engagement: A Note to Leaders

The frameworks and strategies provided in this guidebook are designed to promote positive growth across multiple layers: the personal, the professional, and the organizational, which function within the context of the larger societal/structural dimension (see figure 3). Vibrant schools that address structural inequities and strive to serve the needs of all children in a diverse, multiracial society are essential to maintaining and advancing democracy. This fourth structural layer is where we see the culmination of our efforts at scale and over time. This is the essential long-term work that we do through our professional associations, our local and state-level networks, and our personal advocacy. Historically, societal influences have played a pivotal role in advancing the social justice and equity agenda at key moments (Brown v. Board of Ed). However, at other periods, as we are experiencing at the time of this writing, the political climate has been highly regressive. Much of the work we do every day in our classrooms is nurturing the next generations of engaged citizens committed to the values of pluralistic democracy. This is the deeper work that undergirds the Empowered Stewardship approach. We cannot transform our schools without transforming our practices, and we cannot transform our practices without transforming ourselves. And the entire process of transformation must be supported at the societal/structural level.

Figure 3: Layers of Engagement

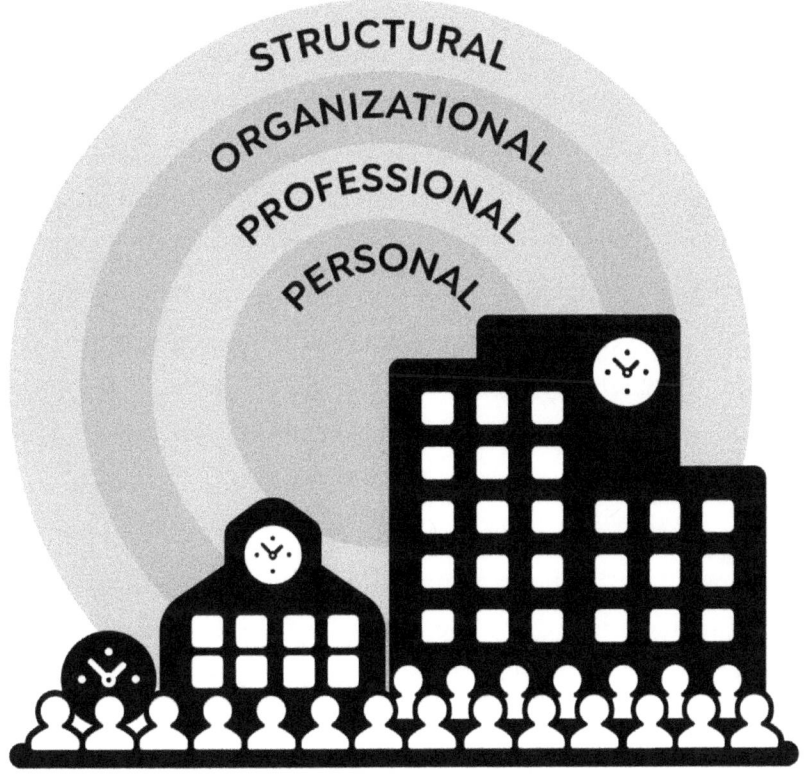

"Changing systems requires changing people, and changing people requires changing systems (Fullan, 2016)." Thus, as shown in Figure 3, our work must flow across all four layers and in both directions, from the outside in and from the inside out. Achieving a greater degree of inclusion, equity, and excellence in our schools requires transformative work that is both multidimensional and multidirectional.

It should come as no surprise that the top-down, large-scale school reform efforts in recent decades failed to meet their stated objectives. Both *No Child Left Behind* and *Race to the Top* were planned and executed from the socio-political arena (see the outer circle on Figure 3) and were heavily influenced by the business community, as well as major foundations and think tanks. Most notably, these efforts lacked any meaningful participation of actual teachers and school leaders. The resulting mandates were then imposed monodimensionally and monodirectionally on the schools. The assumption, based on a corporate business model, has been that these externally driven incentives and punitive consequences would lead to positive change in school outcomes, professional practices, and the personal buy-in and motivation of educators.

This market-driven approach has clearly not worked, and many have argued that it actually disproportionately harmed our most marginalized students (Gorski & Zenkov, 2014; Ravitch, 2013; Schniedewind & Sapon-Shevin, 2012). The roots of this approach can be traced to the reauthorization of the Elementary and Secondary Education Act (ESEA) as No Child Left Behind (NCLB) in 2001, which codified the belief that standardized test scores were the ultimate indicator of school, teacher, and student success. This policy shift, steeped in federal accountability mandates, enshrined a narrow definition of achievement and tied it to punitive consequences, particularly for schools serving low-income communities, English learners, and students of color. Although the most recent reauthorization of ESEA, the Every Student Succeeds Act (ESSA) of 2015, reduced some of the high-stakes consequences and returned more decision-making to states, it maintained the central role of standardized testing in evaluating school performance.

One example of such top-down reasoning was the Measures of Effective Teaching project, funded by the Bill & Melinda Gates Foundation to the tune of $45 million (Gabriel & Allington, 2012). The entire effort suffered from a flawed assumption that, unfortunately, was also the guiding principle of the No Child Left Behind era under ESEA, that the ultimate measure of a teacher's effectiveness is reflected in student test score gains. Even though the researchers argued that they also considered other measures such as classroom observations and student feedback, the test score (or "value-added score" to use another term from the business world) was the gold standard against which all other measures were vetted.

This being the case, they then hypothesized that the end-all strategy to level achievement gaps (a problematic concept to begin with) was a simple matter of identifying "best practices" and holding teachers accountable for implementing them by using more sophisticated teacher evaluation tools. It should come as no surprise to those of us who spend our days in real schools with real students that, at the end of the day, there were no significant achievement gains in the schools that participated in the study. Moreover, one can see how such efforts to distill "effective teaching" down to a narrow set of "best practices" are incongruent with a basic understanding of equity. It would be an instructive thought experiment to ponder how that $45 million investment could have been alternatively used.

We have no doubt that teachers can have a powerful influence on students' lives, but such carrot-and-stick solutions to improving our schools rarely acknowledge the deep-rooted, structural inequities that are the most significant barriers to success for marginalized students (the outer circle of the Layers of Engagement design). With tragic predictability, race and poverty continue to determine dropout rates, discipline referrals, and learning outcomes for far too many of our nation's historically underserved and most marginalized students (Ravitch, 2013).

Borrowing from the language of brain research, we want our teachers and leaders to arrive at a place of neuroplasticity (Wexler, 2006), which speaks to our ability to create new neural pathways and modify existing ones. We can make this happen when we enter a state of mental and emotional flexibility that allows us to examine how we think and act relative to our professional practices, and to consider alternative approaches. The activities, discussion, and conceptual frameworks in this guidebook have been proven effective in inviting educators to *willingly*, not coercively, enter this courageous self-reflective space. This state of self-generated neuroplasticity provides the productive foundation from which to critically assess how we relate to our students across the many dimensions of difference, including race, ethnicity, language, gender identity, sexual orientation, social class, and neurodiversity.

The work begins with self-examination, but the Stewardship approach offers many strategies for moving the work from the personal to the professional, and from the professional to the organizational layers of engagement. As leaders, our responsibility is not only to guide our faculty and staff into the process of personal and professional growth but also to create the kind of school culture and organizational practices that will support and sustain them in this transformative work.

The Four A's

The Four A's create an opportunity for conversation and reflection during your Stewardship journey. Once learned, they provide you with four areas to focus ongoing discussions, planning, and implementation.

Alignment

Does the idea of a Culture of Stewardship align with your current mission, vision, and strategic goals? Assure that the Stewardship work is connected to and supportive of your school/district foundational elements. Ensure that the work is connected to previous equity and inclusion efforts and other ongoing programs/approaches to avoid duplication of efforts and the perception of isolated initiatives.

Accountability

Across all levels of the organization, do individuals and teams have the Stewardship work integrated into planning, implementation, and goal-setting efforts? What evidence will they gather to know their impact? Leaders at the district and school levels need to be engaged in continuous improvement conversations related to their Stewardship goals and outcomes and have evidence of results built into their professional growth plans and performance reviews.

Assessment

Are there regular check-ins and ongoing review processes in place to track and document YES outcomes across all levels of Stewardship engagement (personal, professional, and the organization)? How can action plans be consistently tracked, assessed, and updated?

Advocacy

Are all members of the community actively engaged and represented in the YES process? Are the concerns of the traditionally marginalized listened to and effectively addressed so they can be empowered stewards for the community? In the Stewardship process, particular attention is given to students, employees, families, and members of the community who have been marginalized, excluded, or not effectively served by the school or district.

What are you thinking? What do you want to remember?

Part 4: Engaging in Collaborative Inquiry

Inquiry is at the heart of Empowered Stewardship. This chapter introduces the YES Collaborative Inquiry Process, which is a dynamic, liberatory model that integrates evidence, empathy, and creativity to transform reflection into systemic action. Grounded in human-centered-liberatory design, YES inquiry engages both students and adults as co-designers of just, inclusive learning environments.

You'll explore how YES builds on and expands the Impact Teams Collaborative Inquiry model by anchoring inquiry in relational trust, shared leadership, and community expertise. The chapter introduces a cyclical process that guides participants through noticing inequities, deepening awareness, co-creating solutions, and sustaining equity-driven transformation.

You'll also learn about the Five Streams of Engagement, which provide a responsive structure for embedding inquiry into every layer of school life—personal, professional, team, and organizational. Each stream supports a distinct aspect of equity-centered transformation, from building relational foundations and honoring lived experience to dismantling systems of dominance and cultivating creative resistance. These streams will be explored in greater detail in Section Two, but this chapter offers an essential introduction to how collaborative inquiry activates and sustains a culture of Stewardship in your school community.

The YES Collaborative Inquiry Process

The Youth Empowered Stewardship collaborative inquiry model is where theory meets practice and evidence informs action, ensuring that inquiry is not just reflective but transformative. The YES inquiry model evolves from and builds upon decades of design-based educational change efforts, drawing first from human-centered design principles (Brown, 2009; Roschuni et al., 2013) and later integrating the critical stance and equity orientation of liberatory design (Tucker-Ray et al., 2016).

The YES collaborative inquiry anchors its model in liberatory design, a framework co-developed by Anaissie, Clifford, Wise, Cary, and Malarkey in collaboration with the National Equity Project (Anaissie et al., 2021). Liberatory design intentionally integrates empathy, iteration, and co-creation by shifting the balance of power and actively engaging communities most impacted by injustice. Through this stance, YES explicitly surfaces power dynamics, honors lived experiences as essential expertise, and fosters equity-centered collaboration to transform unjust systems. By embracing liberatory mindsets, such as recognizing oppression, cultivating deep self-awareness, and prioritizing relational trust, and applying iterative, reflective processes (National Equity Project, n.d.), YES ensures that the voices guiding systemic change belong to those historically marginalized or excluded.

The YES Inquiry model integrates seamlessly with the Impact Team Collaborative Inquiry approach (Bloomberg, Pitchford, & Wells, 2025), as both frameworks anchor their methodologies in liberatory design—a process that intentionally surfaces power dynamics, honors lived experiences, and actively transforms inequitable systems through empathy, iteration, and co-creation (National Equity Project, n.d.). The Impact Team model specifically advances instructional excellence by fostering agency in every learner, emphasizing culturally responsive assessment practices that elevate learner voice and ensure continuous improvement. This collaborative inquiry model uses structured cycles of evidence-based reflection and collective decision-making to create equitable learning environments where all students thrive. By grounding their inquiry processes in liberatory design, YES and Impact Teams empower educators and communities not only to identify and address systemic inequities but also to build sustainable, justice-centered educational systems that uphold equity, dignity, and agency for all learners.

From Reflection to Liberation: A Cyclical Process

At its core, YES engages in parallel and mutually reinforcing cycles of inquiry, ensuring that both professional learning and student-led inquiry drive system-wide change. This six-phase model follows an iterative, liberatory design thinking process (see Figure 4) that challenges oppression in education and fosters co-agency (Tucker-Ray et al., 2016). Once learned, it can be used for the rest of an educator's or team's career to tackle any issue.

> **Notice & Disrupt:** Pause to observe, reflect, and uncover hidden inequities in learning experiences and school structures. Amplify historically silenced voices and challenge dominant narratives.
>
> **Empathize & Deepen Awareness:** Gather qualitative and experiential evidence by listening deeply to students, families, and communities. Honor nondominant stories that illuminate systemic barriers.
>
> **Define & Reframe:** Triangulate empathy-driven insights with schoolwide data. Reframe challenges to address root causes rather than symptoms.
>
> **Ideate & Imagine Beyond Constraints:** Reject limitations. Embrace creativity to innovate. Design bold, justice-driven possibilities that transcend compliance and disrupt systems to cultivate liberatory futures.
>
> **Prototype & Co-Create:** Shift from ideas to action. Test, refine, and iterate strategies that center justice, learner agency, and collective power.
>
> **Evaluate & Sustain:** Assess impact through an equity lens. Identify how power shifts in decision-making and ensure continuous co-design with students and families.
>
> **Transforming Schools Through Inquiry & Liberation**
>
> By weaving liberatory design principles into collaborative inquiry, the YES model moves beyond equity as an abstract goal and instead fosters sustained, justice-driven transformation. This approach ensures that schools don't just "include" marginalized voices; they center and amplify them, actively dismantling oppressive structures and co-creating new, liberatory learning ecosystems.

Figure 4: The Design Thinking Process

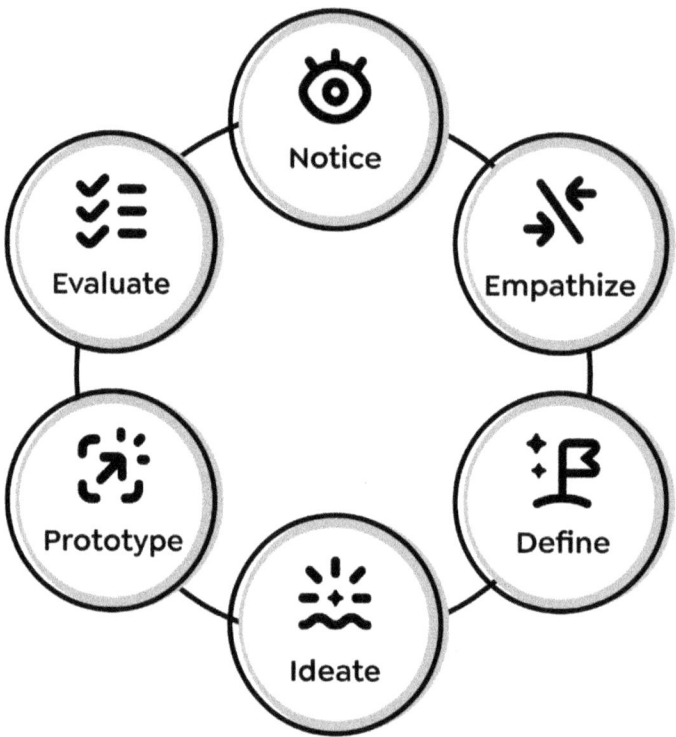

Source: Bloomberg & Pitchford, 2023.

The YES collaborative inquiry process grounds each cycle in the *Achievement Triangle* and is informed by the *Seven Stewardship Commitments*, both of which were addressed in Part 3, and will be expanded upon later in this guidebook. Collectively, they serve as powerful anchors, ensuring that inquiry is not just about intervention, but about creating learning environments where every student belongs and thrives. YES collaborative inquiry creates intentional spaces for co-constructing equitable learning experiences that honor identity, belonging, and justice.

In practice, this process is both cyclical and non-linear. While the model outlines a clear sequence of phases, teams revisit earlier steps as new insights and voices emerge. Based on examples from our work, a team may begin by noticing that Native students are frequently absent from school and move forward with strategies based on surface-level assumptions. However, after gathering empathy-driven input from families, they may learn that students attend school on a nearby reservation one or two days each week. This disrupts attendance patterns in the public school system and reveals a deeper cultural and structural issue. In response, the team pauses, returns to earlier phases, and deepens their understanding by inviting Tribal elders to co-lead learning opportunities for staff and students. Rather than progressing in a straight line, the inquiry evolves through reflection, relationship-building, and cultural responsiveness.

This kind of iteration is essential. A team might launch a theory of action to better support Pacific Islander students, only to discover during implementation that other student groups face related challenges. Instead of closing the loop, the team returns to the *Notice and Disrupt* phase to expand their focus and adjust their approach. In this way, inquiry becomes a living, adaptive process that grows with the learning community it serves.

Student-led efforts in Patterson, Auburn, and Palm Springs also reflect the ongoing, expansive nature of this work. In these districts, and more, students investigated critical issues, from cultural invisibility to safety concerns, and designed solutions in collaboration with peers, educators, and community members. As their projects evolved, students and adults alike circled back to listen more deeply, gather new perspectives, and refine their actions.

This process is more than a change strategy. It is a liberatory practice that centers community knowledge, fosters continuous reflection, and sustains equity-driven transformation over time and far beyond the walls of the school building.

As your team prepares to launch its own inquiry cycle, we encourage you to study the narrative below and the examples in the back of this guide.

What Your Team Will Need to Get Started with Inquiry

To support your team's use of this process, a full YES Collaborative Inquiry template is available in the back of this guidebook. The template guides your team step-by-step through the process, from identifying a puzzle of practice to designing equity-centered solutions. You will also find "snapshots" that demonstrate a stripped-down version of the inquiry process so you can begin to generalize the thinking required in each phase.

- What to bring when you start:
- Demographic data
- State-level performance data (SBA, CAASP, etc.)
- Screener and diagnostic data (Star, i-Ready, MWEA Map, Acadience, etc.)
- Multilingual learner data (i.e., WIDA)
- Attendance data
- Behavioral and discipline referral data
- School climate data (i.e., Panorama)
- Any extant student voice data

The YES Collaborative Inquiry Process in Practice

Often, the best way to understand a complex process is to see it in action. When that's not possible, studying an example is the next best thing.

The YES Collaborative Inquiry Process is not a linear checklist, but a dynamic, iterative cycle of liberatory learning and leadership. Each of the six phases invites teams to shift power, amplify historically silenced voices, and center justice in the co-creation of equitable learning environments based on the school's strengths and opportunities with the Seven Stewardship Commitments.

The details in the narrative below are grounded in the real challenges, questions, and insights we have encountered in our work with schools and illustrate what a school might do when committed to equity and student voice. We hope you find this a useful model for learning and planning.

Madrona Middle School's Story

Madrona Middle School is in a large suburban school district in the Pacific Northwest. The district demographics have changed significantly over the past 20 years, as they have welcomed increasingly diverse immigrant students and families from conflict zones and distressed global communities over the past 7 years. The district serves a large Native American community, some of whom cycle in from the tribal school into public school and back. Madrona serves mostly lower-income students and families. The district has invested in equity and inclusion professional development and adopted frameworks and classroom practices over a decade. These efforts have resulted in the achievement of level 1- 4 YES outcomes (see Part 2 above) to varying degrees in buildings across the district. The following narrative represents the first year Madrona Middle School adopted and implemented the YES Collaborative Inquiry Cycle process. The school has a long-term principal and vice principal and has a history of retaining staff. The leadership team has expressed the need to hire and retain more staff of color who might better represent the diversity in the building. They have multiple culture clubs. The Pacific Islander (PI) club is one that tends to be very well attended and has proven to be a motivator for students to be more engaged in school.

Table 1: Madrona Middle Demographic Data

Race/Ethnicity		Population Groups	
Alaskan Native/Native American	5%	Multilingual Learners	64%
Asian	8%	Special Needs	16%
Black	9%	504 Plan	4%
Native Hawaiian/Pacific Islander	25%	Free & Reduced Lunch	56%
Hispanic	24%	Notable Changes and/or Historical Trends	
Two or More Races	11%	Over the past five years, the Pacific Islander student population has increased by 45%, with a concurrent rise in multilingual learner (ML) identification. This trend reflects shifting community demographics and highlights the growing need for culturally and linguistically responsive support.	
White	17%		
Total Student Population	875		

Notice and Disrupt

This phase is about looking courageously at your current system. Begin by observing data, student experiences, and school culture to uncover strengths, hidden inequities, and dominant narratives. Use a justice lens to examine not only outcomes, but who benefits, who is harmed, and who is missing from the conversation. The goal is to identify disparities and disrupt the assumptions and structures that sustain them based on analysis of multiple evidence sources.

In looking at the satellite level State Office of Public Instruction (OSPI) report card, the map level district data on attendance, discipline, grade-level readiness and the district's Center for Educational Effectiveness (CEE) parent/student/staff/stakeholder perception data, it became clear fairly soon where their first collaborative Inquiry focus would be at Madrona Middle School.

Native Hawaiian/Pacific Islander (PI) students (many of whom are low-income and multilingual learners) were showing up to school 26% less often than white students. Their math SBA rates and reading scores were 6-10% lower than those of African American students. They were being sent to the office more than any other group, and their CEE data showed that a high number of PI students did not feel a sense of belonging at school. Both their qualitative and quantitative data were trending down for PI students when they were trending upward for most other groups. Through conversations with the equity leadership team and by engaging the *School Climate Assessment* (see Stream 1 Engagements for a detailed description), it became clear that there was a general sense of frustration among staff around not knowing how to find solutions and that there was a general lack of knowledge about Samoan, Martallese, Figian, Tongan, and Hawaiian culture.

We engaged strategies from Streams 2 and 3 – *Culture Toss, We, the People, and the Dynamics of Dominance* (refer to these strategies in the Streams of Engagement for a detailed description), starting with the equity leadership team and expanding to all staff through PLC time in order to begin exploring what adult practices and perceptions might be getting in the way of these kids showing up to school and being successful when they are there. Through listening to colleagues and courageous dialogue, the equity team came to the realization that while their focus had been on finding classroom strategies to solve the problem, the focus needed to be on the Knowing Self and Knowing Students sides of the *Achievement Triangle* because educator bias and stereotypes about how families value education was getting in the way of serving the needs of the PI community.

Empathize and Deepen Awareness

Beyond the data we have readily available in most schools, we must listen deeply. This phase invites you to gather stories, lived experiences, and insights of all students, but especially from those most impacted by inequity.

In this example, the Madrona Leadership team gathered empathetic data from PI students. Empathy helps us uncover root causes, recognize cultural assets, and understand exclusion not as disengagement, but often as resistance or response to injustice. Each of the steps in this phase offers guiding questions to ensure the team's ability to gather insights in ways that are humanizing and culturally responsive.

One of the more exciting moves Madrona Middle School made was to invite students into the conversation early on in the inquiry process. One of the things they noticed in the first stage of inquiry was that, while PI kids were absent a lot, very few students ever missed PI club days. The equity leadership team chose to use some of those days to create opportunities to learn from students about their experience in school, and what might be getting in the way of their success. We created a welcoming space by bringing in students' favorite musicians (this was an incredible opportunity for educators to learn about the lexicon of traditional music and island pop artists). We created space for students to play the ukulele and sing. We provided food and brought in visual art.

The engagement strategies offered were in Streams 2 and 4, focused on the power of personal/cultural story and students' experiences in school spaces; *Community Agreements, In My One Beat, Lenses of Difference, The Desert Monsoon Model,* and *The 7 Stewardship Commitments* (refer to these strategies in the

Streams of Engagement for detailed descriptions). Some of the street-level empathy data we collected from PI students were as follows:

- "Some of our parents don't speak great English, they speak Marshallese, but they don't read Marshallese - so written surveys and invitations don't always work."

- "Asking questions and expecting short answers does not work for us. We tell stories."

- "We need more music, more life in school."

- "We want to have opportunities to work with other clubs and other kids. We have a lot in common with Mexican kids. We want to meet more with them, too."

- "It's not that we're bad at math; some of us just learn differently."

- "We feel like sometimes we're seen as one thing, not all the things that we are."

These sessions were far more than empathy interviews; they were intergenerational experiences where students and adults learned from and with each other. The students reported that they learned a lot and felt empowered as equals. The equity leadership team shifted their focus to a year-long emphasis on *Stewardship Commitments 1-3*, drawing on insights from students. They learned that students needed to feel teachers understood their culture and valued their way of being and learning in order to participate and learn effectively. One student expressed that if she knew that her teacher was even just a little curious about her life and her culture, she would be far more excited about learning. Almost all of the students expressed that they wanted school spaces to be more culturally relevant and vibrant. 100% of the PI group chose family as the most important aspect in their life, and they wanted their families to be more included in school life. In short, these intergenerational learning experiences caused the equity leadership team to gain vital knowledge of student experience and perception, and caused them to shift their professional learning to the Front Porch Commitments (see Stream 4).

Define and Reframe

This stage acts as a bridge connecting deep understanding with meaningful action. During this phase, teams clearly and precisely define their "puzzle of practice," the central challenge you are addressing, by triangulating empathy-driven insights with schoolwide data. The analysis done in the first two phases provides teams with a deeper understanding of the root cause(s) so they can reframe the puzzle of practice based on their new understandings. The Madrona team determined their puzzle of practice based on the evidence generated from phases one and two of the inquiry process.

One of the harder lessons at Madrona Middle came after an invitation was sent out to families to come to an evening event at the school, share a meal, celebrate, and have conversations about students' and families' experiences with school. Many of the families either did not respond or took the time to share that they would not be attending. This sent the equity team back to the students to ask why their families might not want to attend. The following are some of the responses:

- "My parents work at night and I take care of my siblings."
- From a Marshallese student: "We have had really bad experiences with the American education system. Schools are pretty bad in the islands, and the military dropped bombs on us, and that made a lot of our grandparents sick."
- "There's a lack of trust."

The declined invitation and what students said about it reinforced their refocus of professional learning toward the Front Porch Commitments and the Self and Student sides of the *Achievement Triangle*. It also allowed the team to reframe their puzzle of practice away from the problem being defined as something wrong with students and families, and more toward a knowledge/empathy deficit among staff. As the team started to ideate and imagine solutions, it became clear that in order to close an awareness gap amongst staff, they would need to go out into the community to learn, rather than invite families into the school.

Ideate and Imagine Beyond Constraints

In this phase, teams brainstorm equity-centered, evidence-informed possibilities that disrupt business as usual and honor learner voice, identity, and agency. This is where Stewardship meets innovation.

Once the puzzle is clear, it's time to brainstorm possible evidence-based solutions to support the whole learner. What would it look like to build something better, reject limitations, and embrace innovation?

Once again, the Madrona Middle School team went to students so that their ideation and innovation would reflect student perspectives. This second round included the same protocols as round one: democratic room space (chairs in a circle), return to Community Agreements, including music and the arts, movement, and multiple conversation structures. The questions were:

- If there were no limits to possibility, how would school look, sound, and feel to you?
- What do you and your family need from teachers and school leaders to feel you are truly a part of this school community?
- What do we need to know that we don't know now?

Many of the students' contributions and ideas aligned with their earlier desires for school spaces to be more culturally relevant and vibrant. They wanted more content that reflected their own cultural perspective and history. The strategies they developed were based on what the team was already doing that was working, expanding on those innovations, and taking action based on what they learned from students. They saw the ideation step in the inquiry process as a way to synthesize lessons learned from the Self and Students sides of the *Achievement Triangle* and draw them into the Practice aspect.

Prototype and Co-Create

Now we turn ideas into action through collaborative experimentation. In this phase, you'll test, refine, and iterate strategies that center justice, learner agency, and collective power. This process includes creating a theory of action, determining evidence, and setting SMARTIE goals. The process is iterative and designed to test, learn, and revise in partnership with students and families. Justice is not something done to a system; it is built with the people most affected.

The Madrona leadership team reached out to colleagues across the district, brought in allies within the school community, and partnered with students from the beginning of the process. As a result of these connections, many of the team members felt like their Theory of Action was clear, self-evident, and almost wrote itself by the time they reached the Prototype and Co-create phase.

Theory of Action: If we create consistent opportunities for Pacific Islander families to share their stories and goals with school staff, if we create opportunities to go out into the community and learn, and if we empower students to express their culture and identity through advisory and classroom activities, then students will feel a greater sense of belonging, which will lead to improved attendance and classroom participation, which will result in stronger academic outcomes in reading and math for Pacific Islander students.

Questions that were still open at the time of creating this Theory of Action were:

- What specific strategies can we use to authentically invite PI families into dialogue?
- Which community partners can we collaborate with?
- What PI history and social studies resources can we deploy to expand cultural relevance in content?

Evaluate and Sustain

This phase is about trying new ideas, learning from what works and what doesn't, and committing to ongoing change. Measure your impact through multiple lenses, including student experience and power dynamics. Celebrate progress, adjust your approach, and embed what works into your school's culture and systems. Sustainability means ensuring inquiry continues as a way of being, not just a one-time project.

Progress monitor actions, evaluate impact, celebrate success, refine actions, and ensure ongoing co-design with students and families. Ensure you have the equity team you need to maximize impact and make a clear plan for implementing and monitoring your next steps.

The work moving forward at Madrona is around sustaining and growing the PI student club, expanding to make connections across other clubs, building out opportunities for authentic community engagement, and expanding access to culturally relevant curriculum. They are expanding their qualitative, or Street Data (Safir & Dugan, 2021), sources to include student-led assemblies and cultural celebration, intergenerational empathy dialogue, family and community outreach and dialogue, and their CEE climate survey.

Based on the success of their theory of action being informed by students, the Madrona team is also working with students to design their impact assessment. They are also developing opportunities for student YES Ambassadors to be in conversation and lead YES engagement strategies with elementary students.

The Five Streams of Engagement

YES is designed around five dynamic Streams of Engagement (see Figure 5) that evolve responsively throughout the inquiry process. Each stream is intentionally designed to cultivate a school culture where equity is not just an aspiration but a lived practice—one that honors diverse identities, dismantles systemic barriers, and empowers every member of the community to thrive.

The term "Stream" reflects a larger metaphorical structure connecting the work of Stewardship to rivers, water, and natural ecosystems. While Stewardship evolved in classrooms and schools across the United States, Canada, and Australia, it has also developed in the wilderness, specifically on the Colorado River in Grand Canyon National Park. Benjie has worked as a wilderness guide and boatman there for 30 years. Benjie, Wade, Gary, and Patricia have designed and led Stewardship educational expeditions on the Colorado River for teachers, leaders, community activists, and students since 1997. As we are educators, the canyon has become more than a metaphor for us. It is a primary source of knowledge, the ultimate classroom, and a testing ground, where new approaches to engagement have evolved, where we have practiced the very real art of building a multiracial, multiethnic, multifaith, intergenerational community, anchored in stewardship.

Each YES Stream incorporates specific engagement strategies designed to support collaborative, personal, team, and organizational inquiry, aligning closely with the Layers of Engagement detailed in Part 3. For an in-depth exploration of these strategies, please refer to Section Two, which contains five entries, each dedicated to one of the YES streams and their corresponding engagement strategies.

Figure 5: The Streams of Engagement

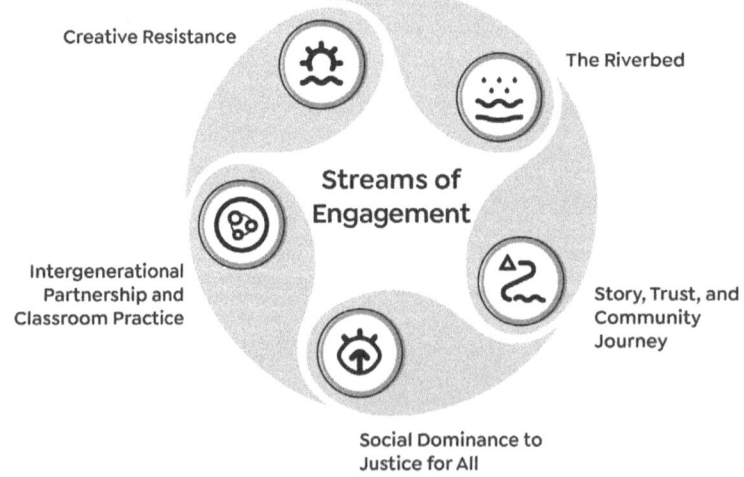

Stream 1: The Riverbed

The Riverbed dimension of the work is about building a strong base over which Stewardship can flow and flourish. Drawing from liberatory and human-centered design, leaders collaborate to envision and prototype cultures steeped in equity, inclusion, and collective excellence. Systemic transformation cannot be enacted by a single leader. It calls for collective engagement and commitment from teams within the school ecosystem to create equitable learning environments where every student and employee, regardless of background or identity, can succeed and flourish. It is dependent on a critical mass of people who are willing and capable of engaging in challenging personal work. As individuals, we translate personal transformation into professional practice. As a collective, we share a willingness to take courageous action within an organization or in the community. We commit to cultivating a belief in the practice of public education as the beating heart of a healthy, sustainable, and vibrant democracy. This foundational work ensures that support is established for adult stakeholders, helpful protocols are used, and appropriate frameworks and expectations are understood and agreed upon.

Stream 2: Story, Trust, & Community Journey

We will never actualize our vision without first establishing trust across our collective. This stream of learning is about building the trust that enables us to be vulnerable with one another by exploring our own personal stories and the stories of others. In doing so, we lay the groundwork for engaging in this courageous work together and to find and celebrate the unity we discover in our diversity. The central aspects of Stewardship are care, knowledge, and action—all of which grow through the expansion of the stories we tell about who we are, where we come from, and the personal histories that have brought us to this moment.

Stream 3: Social Dominance to Justice for All

In addition to sharing our personal stories and histories, another central function of Stewardship is to reflect on the historical roots of inequality. In the words of writer and civil rights activist James Baldwin, *People are trapped in history and history is trapped in them* (1955). In Stream 3, we acknowledge the systemic functions of power and privilege that have created the struggles we face today. We do this through story, through expanding the collective narrative of who we are as a people, as a nation, and as a school system. Utilizing the arts, literature, diverse narratives, and the lived experience of our students, we look at who gets invited to the table of educational excellence and who is excluded, who gets invited to the decision-making table and who doesn't. Stream 3 challenges us to dismantle and disrupt interpersonal and systemic dynamics rooted in dominance, disempowerment, and the erasure of others and to work toward crafting interpersonal and systemic dynamics rooted in shared power.

Stream 4: Intergenerational Partnership & Practice

Stream 4 of the Stewardship process centers on our culturally responsive practices. In this stream, we will be introduced to the Seven Commitments of Stewardship, providing teams with engagement strategies that foster growth in both personal and professional realms. These strategies are particularly focused on the culturally responsive practices we utilize to support equity and inclusion within our school ecosystems. We will explore a variety of activities that offer a foundation for understanding and applying these vital commitments in educational settings. Personal growth will be encouraged through self-assessment and an action research project aimed at deepening our understanding of these commitments. Additionally, collective learning will occur as we emphasize the value of professional learning communities, where educators collaborate to enhance their practice through shared experiences and insights. The engagements in Stream 4 highlight the importance of placing students' voices at the core of educational development, ensuring that teaching practices are not only effective but also equitable and responsive to diverse cultural contexts. Join us as we engage with these strategies to create more inclusive, equitable, and culturally responsive learning environments, informed by both student input and professional collaboration.

Stream 5: Creative Resistance

Harnessing arts-based and experiential methodologies, Stream 5 cultivates creative resistance, empowering students and educators to translate voice into active agency. Creative Resistance is the intentional choice to respond to injustice with creativity, clarity, and care instead of reacting with anger, fear, or avoidance. It transforms harmful moments into opportunities for healing, dignity, and change. Whether in interpersonal interactions or systemic challenges, Creative Resistance uses reflection, artistic expression, and courageous, collective action to challenge oppressive narratives, design human-centered, equitable systems, and plant seeds for a more just future.

Section 2: Exploring the Streams of Engagement

Where Section One lays the philosophical and structural foundation for Empowered Stewardship, Section Two brings the work to life through a series of five dynamic Streams of Engagement. This section equips readers with adaptable strategies and protocols that support collaborative, personal, professional, team, and organizational inquiry and growth. Each Stream is grounded in the belief that equity is not a destination but a daily practice—one cultivated through story, trust, reflection, creativity, and courageous co-leadership.

The Five Streams of Engagement flow from and reinforce the YES Collaborative Inquiry model, offering concrete tools to enact the Seven Stewardship Commitments and operationalize the Layers of Engagement introduced in Section One. The Five Streams include:

- The Riverbed
- Story, Trust, & Community Journey
- Social Dominance to Justice for All
- Intergenerational Partnership & Practice
- Creative Resistance

The Streams of Engagement provide schools and districts with coherent, interconnected pathways for change. Together, they create space for transformation that is not only systemic and strategic but also deeply human. Each stream is both an entry point and an anchor, guiding you to center dignity, deepen belonging, and reimagine what is possible when students, educators, and families lead together.

These Streams are organized to support clarity and action. Each begins with a description of the Stream's purpose, followed by an overview of its engagement strategies, a breakdown of the Layers of Engagement (personal, professional, organizational), and a summary of how these strategies align with collaborative inquiry. Following that are the engagement strategies themselves.

Stream 1: The Riverbed

Building a Foundation Over Which Powerful Stewardship Work Can Flow

"Every great accomplishment starts with a strong foundation, rooted in passion and purpose."
— Maya Angelou

"If you want to go fast, go alone; but if you want to go far, go together."
— African Proverb

The Stewardship process involves actively and intentionally addressing issues of equity and inclusion within educational settings. As described above, the riverbed is an important ecosystem that works to ensure the quality of the river habitat. Just as the riverbed supports diverse life-forms and contributes to ecological balance, schools and the teams within them must collaborate to create environments where every individual thrives. This foundational effort requires teams to work together with a shared purpose, akin to how the components of an ecosystem interact to sustain life. By collectively defining and working toward these shared goals, teams can align their efforts and resources to create a positive and lasting impact on equity and student outcomes. It requires collective agreement and commitment from teams within the school ecosystem to create equitable learning environments where every student and employee, regardless of background or identity, can succeed and flourish.

The engagement strategies in Stream 1 provide opportunities for you and your colleagues to use data to identify personal, professional, and organizational areas of growth and to more effectively guide your allocation of attention and resources to those areas. Team members will work collaboratively to design the action strategies and make the kind of connections that will provide equitable educational opportunities for all students. Teams will identify the successes you have achieved to date in improving your school outcomes, acknowledge the challenges that still await your attention, and design strategies for addressing those challenges. The engagement strategies that have been intentionally embedded in Stream 1 are meant to create the foundation that will guide your team's decisions and directions throughout the Stewardship process.

Overview of Engagement Strategies

Engagement strategies in Stream 1 establish the foundation for all Stewardship work by cultivating the internal readiness and shared purpose needed to pursue equity-centered change. These strategies support the early stages of collaborative inquiry by helping teams build trust, examine personal beliefs, and align professional practice with inclusive values. They encourage individual reflection, team coherence, and organizational clarity, ensuring a strong base for equitable transformation to take root and flow outward. Refer to the table below for the Stream 1 engagement strategies that activate this foundational work.

Layers of Engagement

The Riverbed Engagement strategies in Stream 1 build the base for transformative work by activating personal reflection and professional collaboration through structured inquiry cycles. It would be good at this point in the process to revisit your notes from the Layers of Engagement discussion presented in Section 1, Figure 3. At the personal level, educators engage in courageous self-reflection to examine their own beliefs, biases, and roles in advancing equity. At the professional level, collaborative teams translate those insights into aligned instructional practices and protocols that foster inclusion and belonging. At the organizational level, leaders create the conditions for shared expectations, tools, and frameworks to be embedded into the school's culture. These foundational practices flow outward to challenge and shift broader societal and structural conditions, redefining what excellence and equity look like in public education.

Engagements that Support Collaborative Inquiry

The YES Collaborative Inquiry Process builds on a strong foundation by creating structures for teams to engage in parallel cycles of personal and professional reflection. Through ongoing inquiry, educators develop the collective capacity to notice inequities, deepen understanding, and transform insight into action. The engagements of Stream 1 support multiple phases of inquiry, but are particularly crucial for identifying trends and patterns, enabling you to disrupt the status quo in Phase 1. You will return to many of these engagements to gather new information, deepen understanding, and imagine new ways of working and learning together.

At the personal level, individuals translate their growth and transformation into professional practice. At the team level, collaborative inquiry strengthens relationships, sharpens collective thinking, and aligns actions with shared commitments. At the organizational level, teams take courageous action to shift systems and cultivate public education as the heart of a healthy, sustainable, and vibrant democracy.

Key Inquiry Engagements in Stream 1:

- **The Achievement Triangle:** This will ground your team in a central organizing framework for all professional learning. (All Inquiry)

- **Community Agreements:** Set the foundation for productive collaborative leadership and shared power. (Empathize)

- **School Outcomes Assessment:** Get baseline tone and trust perception data from your team on personal and professional readiness for deep transformative work together. (Notice and Disrupt, Empathize)

- **School Outcomes Assessment and Catalysts for Growth:** Assess where your organization is now within the three recognizable stages of growth, and identify key actions and leadership behaviors for moving toward the transformative leadership stage. (Ideate, Prototype)

- **The four A's and Applying the Four A's:** Provide four areas to consider when planning for implementation and assessing impact (Define, Prototype, Evaluate)

This foundational work ensures:

- Support is in place for adult stakeholders.
- Helpful protocols guide collaboration.
- Frameworks and expectations are clearly understood and embraced.

Table 2: Applying the Engagements of Stream 1 illustrates how collaborative inquiry occurs across personal, professional, and organizational dimensions. Each bullet indicates the connection to the inquiry process and where an engagement applies in the Achievement Triangle.

Table 2: Applying the Engagements of Stream 1

Strategy	Collaborative Inquiry	Personal (Individual)	Professional (Team)	Organizational (System)
The Achievement Triangle	•	•	•	•
Community Agreements	•	•	•	•
Questions to Consider	•	•	•	•
Climate Assessment	•			
School Outcomes Assessment	•		•	•
Stages of Organizational Growth	•			•
Stages for Growth				•
Catalysts for Growth	•		•	•

The Achievement Triangle

"Teaching, like any truly human activity, emerges from one's inwardness, for better or worse. As I teach, I project the condition of my soul onto my students, my subject, and our way of being together. The entanglements I experience in the classroom are often no more or less than the convolutions of my inner life. Viewed from this angle, teaching holds a mirror to the soul. If I am willing to look in that mirror and not run from what I see, I have a chance to gain self-knowledge—and knowing myself is as crucial to good teaching as knowing my students and my subject. In fact, knowing my students and my subject depends heavily on self-knowledge. When I do not know myself, I cannot know who my students are. I will see them through a glass darkly, in the shadows of my own unexamined life—and when I cannot see them clearly, I cannot teach them well. When I do not know myself, I cannot know my subject—not at the deepest levels of embodied, personal meaning. I will know it only abstractly, from a distance, a congeries of concepts as far removed from the world as I am from personal truth."

– Parker J. Palmer

Description

Meeting students' academic and social needs and aspirations requires professional skill sets, the will and ability to build authentic relationships with those who are different from us, and the capacity to know ourselves at a deeper level. Traditional professional development offers depth with regard to professional practice, and often lacks depth regarding opportunities to deepen self-knowledge and awareness of the rich cultural complexities students bring to the classroom. The Achievement Triangle provides a model to guide the microsteps needed to grow one's cultural competence, a guide for intentional decisions to deepen our knowledge of self, of our students, and of our practice (see Figure 6). In addition, the model can guide teams as they make professional development decisions to support growth directed at the identified areas of focus where change is needed. This model, with cultural competence and Stewardship practices at its core, can guide your work throughout the Stewardship journey. Like a three-legged stool, each side of the Achievement Triangle must be engaged in order for balanced and stable growth. The reflective journey to know self and understand how we show up in the classroom with our students benefits the entire ecosystem of relationships and learning. As stewards of these systems, we intentionally engage in a deeper journey to know those we serve in order to support their growth.

The Achievement Triangle model can be used throughout your work with the Stewardship process and will be referenced in several learning engagements to provide a conceptual framework that can guide personal and professional growth toward cultural competence. Throughout the Stewardship process, there will be several learning engagements that support growth in each side of the Achievement Triangle:

Learning Intentions

- Provide a unified model to guide the overall journey of Stewardship
- Identify personal and professional areas of strength and opportunities for growth

Figure 6: The Achievement Triangle

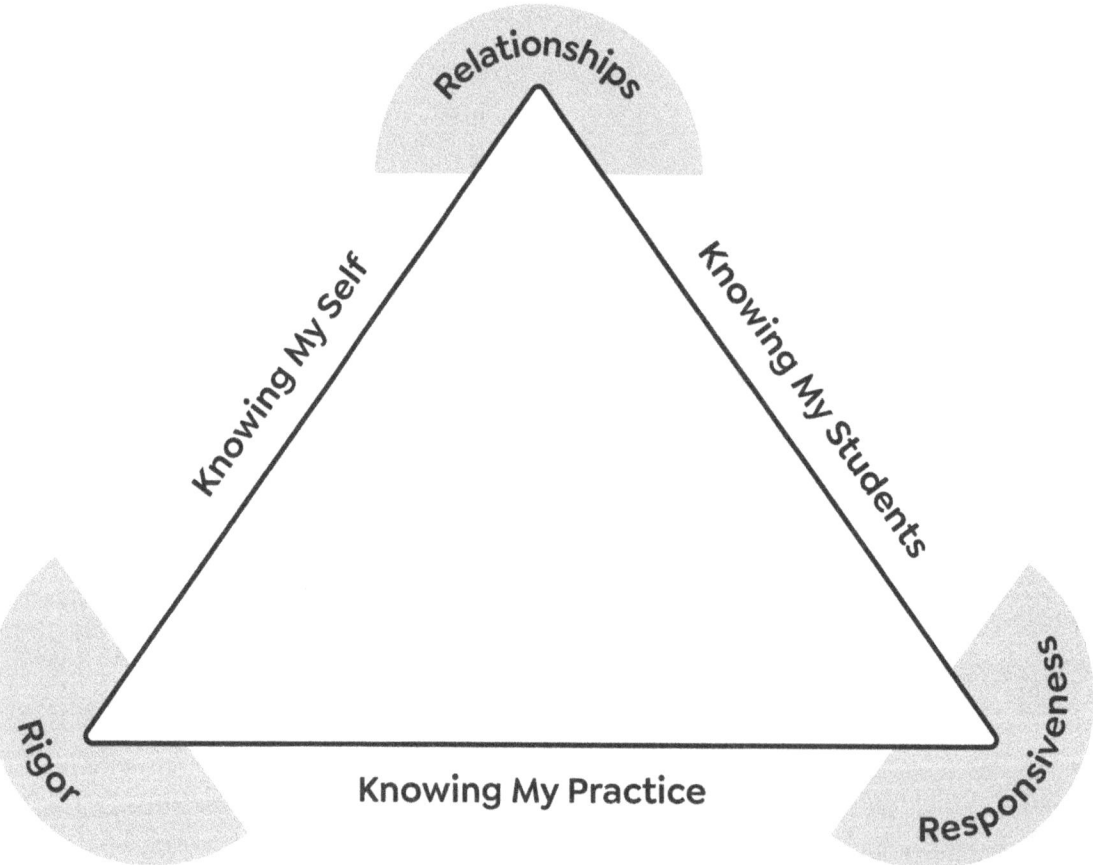

Small Group Discussion

Know Self

- What opportunities have you had in your professional learning experiences to deeply explore and expand your self-knowledge—the experiences, beliefs, and cultural lenses through which you see the world?

- Have you had opportunities to explore how your cultural ways of being are experienced by your students?

Know Students

- How much professional training was focused on the cultural realities, experiences, and ways of being and learning that your current students bring to the school/classroom?

- What types of professional learning have you received that focus on learning about the cultural realities, experiences, and ways of being and learning that your students bring to the school/classroom?

Know Practice

- To what extent does your professional learning and your expertise accommodate for your own cultural experience and ways of being and learning?

- How is your professional expertise connected to your knowledge of students' lives, cultural realities, and ways of being and learning?

Questions to Consider

"Not everything that is faced can be changed, but nothing can be changed until it is faced."
— James Baldwin

Description

This activity provides a good opening conversation, focusing on multiple perspectives regarding issues of equity and social justice that can coexist within the members of a team. This engagement is designed to allow for maximum participation and sharing of ideas with minimum risk, political correctness, or notions of right and wrong opinions. This is meant to be an open-ended activity and used in one of the first engagements in the Stewardship process. This engagement can be helpful when sharing the Equity Team Collaborative Inquiry Plan with the larger school community.

Learning Intentions

- Create a shared space for honest, open-ended conversations about equity and justice
- Recognize and respect multiple perspectives through listening to colleagues
- Record thinking about the long road to equity and social justice
- Shift beyond the shame and blame approach

Given All of Our Efforts to Achieve Educational Equity:

1. Why so long?

2. What's in the way?

3. What will it take?

Personal Reflection

Know Self
- What is something you learned about yourself during this conversation?

- How did your own identity, beliefs, or experiences shape your responses?

Know Team
- What perspectives shared by others helped you think differently or more deeply?

- Where did you hear resonance or divergence?

Know Practice
- What lessons from this dialogue can inform your school's work toward equity, inclusion, and belonging?

- How might these insights influence your teaching, leading, or learning in the weeks ahead?

Climate Assessment

"Trust is the glue of life. It's the most essential ingredient in effective communication. It's the foundational principle that holds all relationships."

– Stephen Covey

Description

Building and nurturing positive interpersonal connections within our educational ecosystems lays the groundwork for personal, professional, and organizational transformation. This engagement encourages all teams to have an awareness of how individually and collectively members are feeling about their interpersonal and professional climate. This information will be essential in creating school spaces where everyone can thrive. Teams are encouraged to consistently invest and assess their efforts toward creating authentic and caring relationships, where all members feel valued and supported. The data collected can then be used to stimulate discussions regarding the school climate and to plan next steps for building a healthier climate that affirms and supports students, families, staff, and the community. Improving relationships across differences is the indispensable prerequisite to meaningful structural changes. Assessments of the climate should happen regularly and often. The following engagement strategy provides an example of a way to check the climate of your educational ecosystem, engaging all stakeholders: teachers, administrators, support staff, students, families, and community.

Learning Intentions

- Assess your current climate with regard to authentic and caring relationships
- Engage in conversation about what needs to happen next to improve your climate
- Gather baseline data to inform planning and measure progress over time

Figure 8: Climate Assessment

To what extent have we created a climate of trust and authentic relationships that allow for real conversations about difficult topics?
Low   High   1   2   3   4   5   6   7   8   9   10

- What are the catalysts that have supported creating a culture of authentic engagement?

- What barriers have gotten in the way?

- What is the story that this assessment data tells us?

Personal Reflection

Know Self

- How do you currently foster authentic engagement with your colleagues and students?

- What do you do to build trust and connection in your everyday interactions?

Know Team

- How does your team foster a climate of inclusion for students, for families, and for one another?

- Where are the strengths in your team's culture? Where are the gaps?

Know Practice

- What do you feel is missing or most needed next to improve your school climate?

- What actions might help build a stronger foundation of trust and care across your school community?

School Outcomes Assessment

"They who fail to plan, plan to fail."

– Proverb

Description

What are the equity-centered outcomes to which we aspire? Where have we already succeeded, and what can we do better? Who are we serving, and who are we not? These questions are both humbling and challenging, but until we address them, and until we agree on a plan to achieve our goals, we are unlikely to make much progress. This engagement strategy will be an essential tool to help you focus on the multiple levels of equity work needed in your school or district. It engages your leadership teams, departments, and buildings in thinking about your effectiveness in reaching the broadest range of students in your school. Through it, we enlist multiple perspectives and we learn how to listen to each other. It calls for nothing less than an honest assessment of your individual and collective effectiveness, and will surface a broad spectrum of perceptions and opinions. Together, you will identify where you are doing a great job with some of your students and where you are missing or not engaging others. The information you gather through this engagement will be useful in guiding your team's actions throughout the Stewardship process. It is suggested that you carry out this conversation with a variety of audiences, including students, to get the broadest picture possible to focus your Stewardship work going forward. It will also be helpful to revisit this engagement from time to time and use that input to assess your progress toward working more effectively with those students you have been missing or not engaging with.

Learning Intentions

- Record critical reflections on the effectiveness of your current practices through an equity lens
- Recognize and explore the range of perspectives among faculty and staff
- Identify students who are well-served and those who are being missed or not engaged
- Establish priority focus areas to guide your next steps in Stewardship planning

Think

1. In our school, we are doing a great/good job with _____-% of our students.
   Characteristics of these students:

2. We are not engaging or missing the mark with _____% of our students.
   Characteristics of these students:

Share

⇨ Discuss the range of your team's answers.

⇨ How similar or different were the perspectives of those in your team?

⇨ How do the characteristics of students in the first group differ from those in the second?

3. Select three groups of students you identified as "not engaging/missing the mark" that you want to be the priority focus for your Stewardship efforts. There are no right or wrong answers here. The value in identifying these students now is in getting a baseline measure of educator perspective. We will return to these lists later, identify where professional perception and data intersect, and make decisions collectively about where your focus will be in the Collaborative Inquiry process.

- _____
- _____
- _____

Personal Reflection

Know Self

- What lessons, insights, or perceptions emerged for you?

- Reflect on your personal level of success with the groups collectively identified as not engaged.

Know Students

- What social dynamics impact the conditions of the students not being engaged?

- How can student voice be included in future assessments of engagement and outcomes?

Know Practice

- What systems currently support efforts to engage students from identified priority groups?

- What barriers exist that limit your ability to engage these students effectively?

- What specific next steps will you take to impact the identified groups?

Stages of Organizational Growth

Description

This engagement strategy introduces your team to a conceptual model for understanding and assessing the equity and belonging culture of your school or organization, as well as examining the power dynamics at work in determining your overall climate of inclusion. *Stages of Organizational Growth* is a developmental model offering a positive focus on your accomplishments to date, as well as an invitation to honestly examine those things that are in the way (see Figure 9). The model brings attention to five arenas of organizational life:

- **Level of Self-Awareness**—how we see ourselves as an organization with respect to diversity and inclusion

- **Emotional Responses to Differences**—how we and our colleagues feel when we engage in discussions of difference

- **Mode of Cultural Interaction**—how we interact with each other across the broad range of differences

- **Approach to Teaching and Learning**—how our pedagogy and curriculum honor the diversity and lived realities of our students, employees, and families

- **Approach to Leadership**—how our leaders use their power. Is it in an autocratic manner ("My way or the highway.") or a collaborative manner ("How can we work together to make the best decisions for our children and community?")?

Related to these arenas, three stages of organizational culture and climate are described in the stages model:

- the *Compliant Stage*, which is characterized by conformity, avoidance of equity issues, and top-down leadership,

- the *Performative Stage*, which is characterized by impressive rhetoric but only a surface-level or performative commitment to equity and belonging, and

- the *Transformative Stage*, which is characterized by a deep institutional commitment to social justice and the transformation of both ourselves and our educational practices.

Section 2: Exploring the Streams of Engagement

Stewardship facilitators will introduce this model as a tool for assessing your current culture and identifying Catalysts for Organizational Growth—policies, practices, and beliefs that can help shift your system toward a more inclusive and equitable Stage 3 culture.

Learning Intentions

- Use a conceptual framework to examine organizational growth toward equity and inclusion
- Explain how school change is a developmental process with recognizable stages
- Assess current organizational culture and climate through the lens of the three Stages of Organizational Growth

Figure 9: Stages of Organizational Growth

	STAGE 1: COMPLIANT	STAGE 2: PERFORMATIVE	STAGE 3: TRANSFORMATIVE
Level of Self-Awareness	Our perspectives are right (the only one)	Our perspectives are one of many	Our perspectives are changing and being enhanced
Emotional Responses to Differences	Fear Rejection Denial We're all alike	Interest Awareness Beginning Openness	Appreciation Respect Joy Enthusiasm Active curiosity
Mode of Cultural Interaction	Isolation Avoidance Hostility	Integration Interaction Beginning Acceptance	Transforming Internalizing Rewarding Challenging Allies
Approach to Teaching and Learning	Assimilation Conformity "Be like us."	Learning *about* those who are "different" Voyeuristic	Learning *from* and *with* all of us Reflective Engaging
Approach to Leadership	Monocultural Autocratic Directive Controlling	Compliance "Image" over Substance "Managing" Diversity	Collaborative Inclusive Empowering *Leading* for Equity

Team Discussion

Reflect on each stage by identifying current indicators in your organization. Discuss with your team and record specific examples that reflect your experience.

Stage 1: Compliant Evidence	Stage 2: Performative Evidence	Stage 3: Transformative Evidence

Personal Reflection

Know Self
- After participating in this activity, which stage do you believe your organization is primarily in? Why?

- What emotions came up for you during this conversation?

Know Team
- What was the tone or feeling in the room as your team explored this model together?

- To what extent did the conversation feel honest and meaningful?

Know Practice
- What lessons or insights emerged about your current culture and where growth is needed?

- What specific actions would you like to take—or see your colleagues and students take—as a follow-up to this activity?

Catalysts for Growth

"The secret of change is to focus all of your energy, not on fighting the old, but on building the new."

— Socrates

Description

The only constant in our world is change. Our ability to lean into a growth mindset and intentionally grow our skills and abilities is part of our personal work as we seek to meet the ever-evolving needs of our current and future students. Likewise, at the organizational level, our journey toward inclusion, equity, and excellence is about enhancing our collective capacity for systemic transformation. We do so by devising and drawing from an array of effective systemic strategies and organizational practices. These institutional efforts are how we shape our collective journey and cultivate our culture of Stewardship. As we discussed in the previous engagement, our approach to school transformation is rooted in an understanding that change unfolds in *Stages of Organizational Growth*. After having assessed your school system's journey relative to these three stages, this next engagement invites you to identify the key *Catalysts for Organizational Growth* that have brought you to your current place, as well as exploring those catalysts that can take you to the next level and support you and your team as you chart a course for future growth.

As you initiate the *Catalysts for Growth* conversation with your colleagues, it is important to acknowledge that the work toward creating a climate of equity and inclusion has already been taking place throughout the district. In this activity, we celebrate the progress that has been achieved so far and identify those catalysts for change that can carry your work to the next level.

This engagement is necessarily linked to *Stages of Organizational Growth* and to the assessment that was part of that conversation. It can also be linked to your *School Outcomes Assessment* conversation and the student identity groups you are missing or not engaging with. By naming both the gains and the challenges, you can develop a more focused and actionable strategy for continued growth. For this conversation, choose grouping structures that best allow for open sharing, collaboration, and learning.

Learning Intentions

- Recognize and celebrate the catalysts that have driven progress toward inclusion, equity, and excellence
- Identify key areas for future growth based on current gaps and missed opportunities
- Align catalysts for change with student populations that have not been effectively engaged or supported
- Continue approaching school change as a developmental process rooted in stages of organizational growth

Personal Think: In your school or district, what have been the most powerful catalysts for inclusion and equity—those things that have helped move you, your colleagues, and your organization toward Stage 3 beliefs, behaviors, and outcomes?

Small Group Conversation

- Describe and discuss the catalysts you have observed/experienced/created in your school. Look for the connections and the differences in your stories.
- List the team actions that support inclusion and equity on the Catalysts Recording Sheet.
- After your list has been created, go through each item and discuss as a team where they fit in the Catalysts for Organizational Growth (see Figure 10).
    ⇨ What are you learning about your past efforts toward inclusion and equity?
    ⇨ What possible future actions are being identified through this conversation?

Figure 10: Catalysts for Organizational Growth

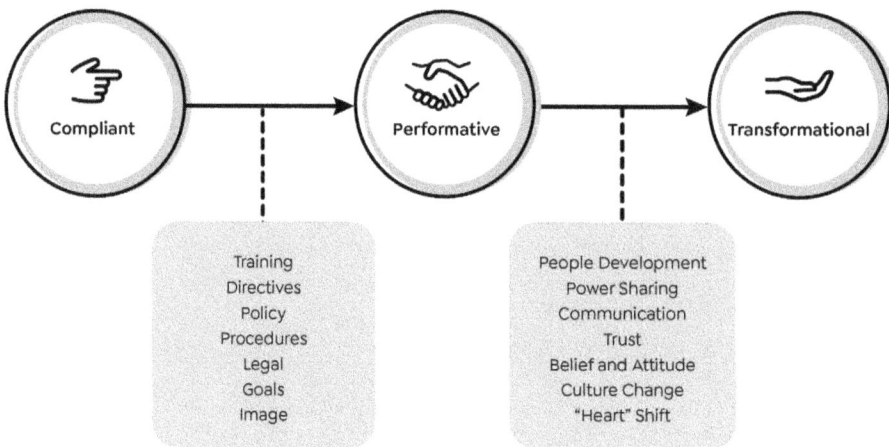

Personal Reflection
Know Self
- What feelings came up for you during this conversation about growth?

- How did your emotional response compare to how you felt during the Stages of Organizational Growth discussion?

Know Team
- Were your reactions similar to or different from those of your teammates?

- How are you contributing to your team's growth in this work?

Know Practice
- Are there ways in which your own participation or perspective may be unintentionally limiting your team's growth?

- What can you do to ensure that your contributions support a deeper, more inclusive growth process?

Kudos and Challenges

Description

As stated in the previous engagement activity, it is important to acknowledge that meaningful work around equity and inclusion has already been underway in your school community. Recognizing this effort, no matter how large or small, is a powerful way to honor progress, avoid blame-based thinking, and build trust across your team. The Kudos and Challenges engagement strategy helps teams celebrate the strategies, programs, and actions that have already created positive change while also naming the persistent roadblocks that need further attention.

This process offers a balanced way to elevate what's working and what still needs to evolve in your equity and school improvement efforts. By identifying your "kudos," you spotlight current strengths and successes that are helping to create inclusive, welcoming learning environments. By surfacing "challenges," you bring forward critical insights that can guide future action.

To support honest and generative conversations, choose grouping strategies that encourage openness and trust. Consider encouraging participants to draw on insights from Stream 1 engagements, as well as connections to your *Climate Assessment*, the *Stages of Organizational Growth, Catalysts for Organizational Growth*, and *Co-Responsibility Work Groups*. When done well, *Kudos and Challenges* becomes more than a conversation and serves as a foundation for continuous learning and collective accountability. Think about using this engagement with your team at the beginning of your Collaborative Inquiry process and in preparation for sharing the inquiry work with the larger school community.

Learning Intentions

- Celebrate the actions, practices, and policies that have advanced inclusion and equity in your school or district
- Identify key equity challenges or unresolved barriers that must be addressed to move forward

Small Group Discussion

Kudos

In what ways has our team taken meaningful steps toward creating inclusive, welcoming, and equitable learning and working environments for all students, families, and staff?

- What policies, programs, or practices have led to positive growth?
- Where are we seeing impact for students who have been historically underserved?

Challenges

What are one or two of the major equity-related challenges, unresolved issues, or roadblocks that still need to be addressed?

- Where are we stuck?
- What patterns or persistent barriers are getting in the way of progress?

Looking Ahead

What are some ways we can sustain momentum and keep equity and Stewardship efforts centered in our work?

- How might we maintain accountability over time?
- What structures or routines could help keep the "fire lit"?

Personal Reflection

Know Self
- What is something you learned about yourself through this and other engagements so far?

- Was it easier for you to identify successes or challenges? Why?

Know Team
- What did you learn from listening to others' perspectives?

- How can you support others in holding onto what's working while also leaning into what's hard?

Know Practice
- How do we use what we've surfaced today to inform our next steps?

- What actions can we take to both honor our strengths and address ongoing equity challenges?

The Four As

Description

The Four As is an opportunity for conversation and reflection during your Stewardship journey. It provides you, as a leader, with four questions to continue ongoing discussions, planning, and implementation. The 4As are excellent for focusing both reflection and feedback and driving continuous improvement.. Use each A to continue to check in on your work throughout the journey.

Learning Intentions

- Provide a reflection for guiding ongoing Stewardship planning and implementation
- Connect Stewardship efforts to school and district strategic goals
- Establish shared accountability across all organizational levels
- Ensure that marginalized voices are meaningfully engaged in all aspects of planning and action

Alignment

Does the idea of a Culture of Stewardship align with your current mission, vision, and strategic goals? Assure that the Stewardship work is connected to and supportive of your school/district foundational elements. Ensure that the work is connected to previous equity and inclusion efforts and other ongoing programs/approaches to avoid duplication of efforts and the perception of isolated initiatives.

Accountability

Across all levels of the organization, do individuals and teams have the Stewardship work integrated into planning, implementation, and goal-setting efforts? What evidence will they gather to know their impact? Leaders at the district and school levels need to be engaged in continuous improvement conversations related to their Stewardship goals and outcomes and have evidence of results built into their professional growth plans and performance reviews.

Assessment
Are there regular check-ins and ongoing review processes in place to track and document YES outcomes across all levels of Stewardship engagement (personal, professional, and the organization)? How can action plans be consistently tracked, assessed, and updated?

Advocacy
Are all members of the community actively engaged and represented in the YES process? Are the concerns of the traditionally marginalized listened to and effectively addressed so they can be empowered stewards for the community? In the Stewardship process, particular attention is given to students, employees, families, and members of the community who have been marginalized, excluded, or not effectively served by the school or district.

Applying the Four As
Talk with your team and record evidence of areas where you are presently doing good work and areas where more work is needed.

Alignment
Example: Assuring that the five Streams of Stewardship are integrated with your school goals and the district's framework.

What evidence of progress can we identify in our school or district?

What next steps are needed to strengthen alignment?

Accountability
Example: Assuring that all schools and district instructional departments are integrating the *Seven Commitments of Stewardship* into their planning, goal setting, and professional review processes.

What evidence of progress can we identify in our school or department?

What next steps are needed to build shared accountability?

Assessment

Example: Tracking progress on meeting the targeted goals you set during your *School Outcomes Assessment* planning and your *Personal Growth Projects*.

What evidence of progress can we identify in our school or department?

What next steps are needed to improve assessment and reflection processes?

Advocacy

Example: Assuring that the action planning ideas and goals generated by your Youth Stewardship cohorts are being listened to, validated, supported, and acted upon.

What evidence of progress can we identify in our school or district?

What next steps are needed to strengthen advocacy efforts and community voice?

Personal Reflection

Know Self
- Which of the Four As do you feel is most important for your team? Why?

- Are there any areas where you've been unsure how to contribute or take action?

Know Team
- For which "A" do you think your school or district has the greatest potential to excel? What's the evidence?

- Are there any of the Four As where you sense resistance, hesitation, or lack of clarity? Why might that be?

Know Practice
- How might you expand, adapt, or challenge the Four As template to better meet your team's needs?

- What ideas, concerns, or reflections would you like to bring to your next Stewardship conversation?

Note on the 4 As:
Continue to revisit The Four As when meeting and making decisions for the members of your school community. The 4 A's are particularly effective when paired with other Stewardship engagement strategies such as *School Outcomes Assessment, Stages of Organizational Growth, Catalysts for Organizational Growth, Achievement Triangle, Personal Growth Plans* (see Stream 2), and *Seven Commitments of Stewardship* (see Stream 4).

What are you thinking? What do you want to remember?

Stream 2: Story, Trust, & Community Journey

"Our stories are all we have. The only thing that will ever save us is to learn each other's stories from beginning to end . . . For every life we know, we are expanded. There is no forgiveness without stories. There is no dignity. There is no way to speak in other tongues than that."

– Karen Fisher

This stream of learning is about establishing trust as a foundation for sharing our personal stories. Through this sharing, we can discover and celebrate both our diversity and our unity. The engagement strategies in this stream are rooted in a belief that our stories are everything. We *are* our stories. Each of us is a fluid and dynamic narrative arc that grows from where we've been, where we are now, and who we want to become. The people and events of our lives are essential elements of these narratives.

Neuroscientific evidence reveals that our brains are hardwired for stories (Suzuki et al., 2018). MRI studies reveal that when we listen to stories being told, our brainwave patterns actually begin to mimic those of the storyteller (Renken, 2020). Yet the power of stories, our own and others', is often overshadowed in a world in which figures and "data points" dominate our meaning-making systems and in which deeply personal self-disclosure is the exception to the rule (Lekoko, 2007; Rezvani & Gordon, 2021).

Our beliefs are in our stories, along with our hopes, our fears, our struggles, our ancestors, our cultures, and our traditions. All of our stories woven together form the fabric of our community. Stream 2 strategies allow us to explore who we are together and what we need from one another. They support us in becoming vulnerable and courageous in our creative collaboration. We do this so that more of us, across more of our differences, can share our stories without fear, and so that we, as educators and students, can achieve at higher levels and engage at deeper levels without giving up who we are and without being forced into assimilative spaces.

The two key components of Stewardship are care and knowledge, both of which grow and expand through stories. The more we share our stories, the more we know of ourselves and others. The more we know, the more we gain empathy and care. The more we know and care, the less likely we are to neglect, diminish, or do harm to others. A key challenge in this stream of learning is to transcend the impulse to control the narrative. Most communities have stories that dominate and stories that are rarely heard (or are actively othered and diminished). This challenge will require us to allow for multiple truths to exist simultaneously. For example, Black Lives Matter as a movement is a story about the experience of Black people in Black bodies; it has never meant that White lives don't matter. This false perception, however, exemplifies the fears that often arise when we expand the story of who is included in the *We, the People* engagement strategy in Stream 3. Much of Stream 2 is about embracing that larger "We." Expanding the narrative in this way requires us to be humble, curious, and courageous. Most importantly, it calls upon us to listen. With this in mind, you will see that many of these engagement strategies are excellent for gathering the empathetic data essential to successful collaborative inquiry. The entire set of learning opportunities in Stream 2 is far more about listening than speaking.

Overview of Engagement Strategies

The engagement strategies in Stream 2 strengthen the collective capacity for collaboration by deepening trust through shared storytelling and cultural inquiry. These strategies create the relational conditions necessary for courageous inquiry by inviting vulnerability, listening, and empathy into the process. By integrating personal narratives into professional learning, teams develop a shared understanding of community histories and identities, positioning story as both evidence and catalyst for inclusive change. See the table below for Stream 2 strategies that support this trust-building work.

Layers of Engagement

Stream 2 centers on the power of story to build trust and community across difference. At the personal level, educators reflect on their lived experiences and cultural narratives, making space for vulnerability and connection. At the professional level, teams engage in deep listening to understand students, families, and colleagues, elevating empathy as an essential part of data gathering and decision-making. At the organizational level, shared stories become a catalyst for changing culture, shifting dominant narratives, and creating more inclusive systems. These actions ripple outward to challenge societal and structural norms that have historically marginalized diverse voices and ways of knowing.

Engagements that Support Collaborative Inquiry

The YES Collaborative Inquiry Process reinforces this stream by ensuring that inquiry begins with empathy and lived experience. Gathering evidence includes listening deeply to students, families, and colleagues to understand their perspectives and challenge dominant narratives. In this way, storytelling becomes both data and a tool for designing inclusive, equity-centered practices. Trust builds as we collectively examine our roles and reimagine what's possible.

The YES Collaborative Inquiry Process reinforces this stream by ensuring that inquiry begins with empathy and lived experience. Gathering evidence includes listening deeply to students, families, and colleagues to understand their perspectives and challenge dominant narratives. In this way, storytelling becomes both data and a tool for designing inclusive, equity-centered practices. Trust builds as we collectively examine our roles and reimagine what's possible.

Table 3: Applying the Engagements of Stream 2 lists concrete strategies at the personal, professional, and organizational levels matched to the Achievement Triangle and the collaborative inquiry process. These engagements provide multiple entry points for building cultural competence, deepening connection, and advancing systemic equity through shared learning and action.

Key Engagements in Stream 2:

- **Definition of Stewardship:** Key to understanding the foundational concept of the professional learning journey, and the two key Stewardship aspects of knowledge and care. (All Inquiry)

- **What is Culture?:** Culture can mean a lot of things to different people. This conversation offers an inclusive and focussed common understanding on three levels. (All Inquiry)

- **Lenses of Difference:** An exploration of the complexity and intersectionality of difference. (Empathize)

- **Culture Toss:** This engagement is an experiential exploration of how the Lenses of Difference impact our understanding of history, our worldview, sense of value and professional practice – critical to knowing self, knowing students and knowing practice. (Notice and Disrupt, Empathize, Define)

- **Stages of Growth and Personal Growth Project:** Every professional working through the Empowered Stewardship process should be actively engaged in at least one Growth Project in order to personally and collectively expand awareness of the communities you serve and the care and knowledge necessary to serve them. (Notice and Disrupt, Empathize, Define)

- **In My One Beat:** Grow care and knowledge through story and creative expression. (Empathize)

Section 2: Exploring the Streams of Engagement

Table 3: Applying the Engagements of Stream 2

Strategy	Collaborative Inquiry	Personal (Individual)	Professional (Team)	Organizational (System)
Homelands Conversation		•		•
Definition of Stewardship			•	•
In Lak'Ech		•		•
What Is Culture?	•	•		•
Definition of Cultural Competence	•	•		•
¿Quiénes Somos?		•		•
Lenses of Difference		•		
Identity Triangle		•		•
Culture Toss		•		•
Stereotype Threat Research	•	•	•	
Stages of Personal Growth Toward Cultural Competence		•		
Personal Growth Project		•		
In My One Beat (Personal Journey)		•	•	•

Homelands Conversation

Description

This engagement strategy is an opportunity to explore the complexity and beauty of who we are and where we come from as individuals and as a community. It allows us to acknowledge the first caretakers of the lands we inhabit and celebrate their historic, ongoing, and current stewardship of people and place. It also allows us to acknowledge and celebrate all the *Nican Tlaca*—translated from the Nahuatl language as "People Here Today," who make up our school community. Some of our ancestors came here as immigrants, and some of us are immigrants ourselves. Some of us are descendants of people who were kidnapped or coerced and brought here by force. Many of us have been displaced by factors outside our control, and some of us have been here for thousands of years. The *Homelands Conversation* allows us to root ourselves as individuals and anchor the launch of our collective learning journey to this place, to the history of how we got here, and the many places and cultures we come from.

Learning Intentions

- Honor First Nations Protocol in Land Acknowledgment
- Honor place, connection to place, and culture for all people
- Explore personal and collective connections to land and history

Know the Land

What is a Land Acknowledgment?

A Land Acknowledgement is a formal statement that recognizes and respects Indigenous peoples as original stewards of this land and the enduring relationship that exists between Indigenous peoples and their traditional territories (New England College Personnel Association, n.d.).

Why do we recognize the land?

> *"To recognize the land is an expression of gratitude and appreciation to those whose territory you reside on, and a way of honoring the Indigenous people who have been living and working on the land from time immemorial. It is important to understand the longstanding history that has brought you to reside on the land, and to seek to understand your place within that history. Land acknowledgments do not exist in a past tense, or historical context: colonialism is a current ongoing process, and we need to build our mindfulness of our present participation. It is also worth noting that acknowledging the land is Indigenous protocol."*
> – Council of Three Fires: Ojibwe, Potawatomi, Odawa

Who are the First Nations people in your community?

What do you know about the Land Acknowledgment statement(s) from First Nations people in your community? If nothing or very little, why do you think that is?

Example from one of our Stewardship school districts:

"The Auburn School District exists on Indigenous land. Just as our schools and offices exist along the Green and White Rivers, so too did the Smalkamish, St'kamish, and Skopamish, and other Indigenous people, who lived in places like the large villages of Ilaqo, Soos Creek, and Burns Creek. We acknowledge the ancestral homelands of the descendants of those who became the Muckleshoot Indian Tribe, who were original caretakers of this land, keeping balance and beauty for thousands and thousands of years. We are grateful to respectfully live and work as guests on these lands with the descendants and members of the Muckleshoot Indian Tribe, who have called this land home since time immemorial and forever more."

This land acknowledgment is one small act in recognizing the importance of continuing to care for the land and acknowledge our important relationship with the Muckleshoot Indian Tribe."
– Auburn School District in Washington State in collaboration with the Muckleshoot Tribal Council

Nican Tlaca

Nican Tlaca is an inclusive, traditional Indigenous concept in the Nahuatl language, meaning "We the People Here Today."

Figure 11: Nican Tlaca

Homelands Conversation

When you hear the term "homelands," what is the association or meaning for you personally? What or where are your homelands?

What aspects come to mind? What landscapes, what internal landscapes, what peoplescapes?

What sounds, smells, and flavors come to mind?

As much as you are willing to share, what feelings are associated with this place or places?

Personal Reflection

Know Self
- What places feel most like "home" to you? Why?

- What is your relationship to the land you live on?

- What have you learned about your community?

- What have you learned about this land and its history?

Definition of Stewardship

Description
We offer this definition of Stewardship as a starting point to deepen and broaden our collective understanding of what it means to be a steward and how we go about crafting a Culture of Stewardship in schools. As the culture grows, so should the language around it. It should become more and more reflective of the land, cultures, and languages of where you live. Again, this is a starting point for you to begin crafting a more localized representative understanding of the concept.

Learning Intentions
- Establish our collective understanding of the concept of Stewardship
- Expand our understanding based on multiple perspectives

Stewardship is . . .
> ACTION, rooted in KNOWLEDGE, in CARE of OURSELVES,
> our FAMILIES, HUMANITY, and the LAND.

Small Group Discussion
- How does the definition resonate with you?
- What words stand out and why?
- What would you add or change?
- What words in what languages might help us deepen our understanding of stewardship?

Personal Reflection

Know Self

- Which part of the stewardship definition most aligns with your personal values or lived experience?

- How do you already practice stewardship in your daily life—toward yourself, others, or the land?

- What cultural or family teachings shape how you understand care and responsibility?

Know Students

- What does stewardship look like in your students' lives or communities?

- How might different students define or practice stewardship differently based on their identities?

- What stories of care, resistance, or protection do your students carry?

Know Practice

- How does your current practice reflect a commitment to stewardship?

- In what ways could your school or classroom culture embody stewardship more fully?

- How can you elevate diverse cultural understandings of stewardship in your teaching or leadership?

In Lak'ech

Description

Luis Valdez wrote a poem called "Pensamiento Serpentino" (Serpentine Thought), published via the Chicano theater company El Teatro Campesino, in 1973. The poem was partially inspired by the Mayan philosophical concept of *In Lak'ech,* or "*Tu Eres Mi Otro Yo / You Are My Other Me.*" The poem has been central in the design of ethnic studies, Mexican American studies, or Chicano studies approaches in school districts in Arizona, Texas, and California over the past few decades.

An early audit of the the K–12 Mexican American studies (MAS) program in Tucson Unified School District (TUSD) in Arizona found that, while the dropout rate for Hispanic students was around 48% in the district (56% nationally), 100% of students enrolled in MAS were graduating from high school and 85% were entering college. A subsequent study by the *American Educational Research Journal* found that students enrolled in MAS classes from multiple race and ethnicity groups performed significantly higher in math and reading, as well as achieving higher AIMS (Arizona State standardized tests) scores (Cabrera et al., 2014). Despite the evidence that a significant number of students benefited from the program, the State of Arizona banned MAS classes and the use of "Pensamiento Serpentino" in classrooms in 2010 via State House Bill 2281, essentially claiming that the program was anti-American and might promote racism against White people. The bill and the TUSD governing board's decision to effectively cancel MAS sparked massive student protests and a number of lawsuits. One lawsuit in particular made its way to federal court. The Arizona State ban on ethnic studies was eventually found to be unconstitutional by the 9th Circuit Court in 2017, the decision stating that the ban itself was racist.

The story of MAS in Tucson from 1998 to the present, and similar ethnic studies–based educational movements in the American Southwest, New York, British Columbia, New Zealand, and elsewhere, are worth researching and emulating with regard to how schools can transform, and how world-changing results can be produced in relatively short order (Bonilla, Dee, & Penner, 2021; Dee & Penner, 2016). Our own research is clear that these approaches, which include the introduction of Indigenous literature, practice, history and philosophy, culture and language empowerment, culture-craft, community outreach and engagement, and critical theory and thought, are the most effective ways of achieving meaningful and sustainable opportunity and achievement expansion for Black, Indigenous, People of Color and lower income White students.

We are including a portion of Luis Valdez's poem here in order to explore and unpack its centrality within successful efforts to elevate outcomes, not only for historically underserved children, but for all children. We also offer it as a discussion catalyst to explore why efforts to introduce Indigenous perspectives, Chicano literature, and Mesoamerican philosophy into American public education, while highly successful in shifting outcomes, have been and remain controversial. (The use of *In Lak'ech* in classrooms has been banned in schools across the country.) Most importantly, we offer it up as an opportunity to explore the meaning of the poem itself and its significance with regard to what it means to be an Empowered Steward, and how we craft a culture of Stewardship in schools.

Learning Intentions

- Introduce the concept of *In Lak'ech* into school practice
- Explore the meaning and its implications in growing a culture of Stewardship
- Include an artistic, uniquely Mesoamerican philosophical lens in the ongoing dialogue

Let's offer the poem as a call and response . . .

In Lak'ech
By Luis Valdez

Tú eres mi otro yo. / You are my other me.
Si te hago daño a ti, / If I do harm to you,
Me hago daño a mí mismo. / I do harm to myself.
Si te amo y respeto, / If I love and respect you,
Me amo y respeto yo. / I love and respect myself.

Personal Reflection

Know Self

- What line from the poem speaks most to your personal values or life experiences?

- When have you experienced a time where "You are my other me" guided or challenged your actions?

- Why do you think the poem has been/is controversial in American public institutions?

Know Students

- How might your students connect to the idea of "You are my other me"?

- What cultural or historical knowledge might help students understand the meaning of this poem?

- What risks or discomforts might students feel when engaging with this content?

Know Practice

- Where in your curriculum or classroom culture could *In Lak'ech* be introduced meaningfully?

- How can the ideas in this poem shift how conflict, care, and community are addressed in schools?

- What barriers (structural, political, curricular) might exist in introducing this perspective, and how can you navigate them?

What Is Culture?

"Culture is not just an accessory to our lives; it is the fabric of our existence."
– Edgar Morin

Description

Earlier in this guidebook, we called out culture as the intricate and complex ecosystem of relationships, norms, traditions, and ways of being that make up who we are and how we see ourselves together as a community of people. As educators in today's schools, we are being asked to be knowledgeable about our own and others' cultures and be responsive to the diverse cultures found in our schools. Since many of us didn't get that type of training in teacher education programs, we are often faced with figuring it out on our own. Some educators come from the communities in which they serve, and their ability to be responsive to the cultural ways of being of their students comes naturally. Most teachers in the United States are teaching in schools where the majority of the students come from other cultural foundations than their own. How can we expand on what we know about our students and provide opportunities for them to share who they are in ways that create inclusive classroom environments where we all thrive?

Culture is within us and around us. It influences our perceptions of others, the ways we behave, and the ways we think. The idea that much of what makes up our culture is unseen has been around since the 1970s, described using the iceberg metaphor, which originated with anthropologist Edward T. Hall (1976). Hall suggested that only 10% of our culture is visible, including elements like language and apparel. The other 90% includes more intangible elements such as values and beliefs. More recent work has built on Hall's levels of culture concept, including Professor Nitza Hidalgo's conceptualization of three levels of culture (Hidalgo, 1993), The Concrete, the Behavioral, and the Symbolic, and more recently Zaretta Hammond's understanding of culture, which uses a tree metaphor that depicts surface (leaves), shallow (trunk), and deep (roots) aspects (Hammond, 2014).

In the Stewardship process, our metaphor of the ocotillo plant (see figure 12) illustrates the organic, fluid, and relational nature of our culture, allowing us to discuss all three levels without valuing one over another. Building on the foundations of Hall, Hidalgo, and Hammond, we organize the levels of culture as follows: Flowers as expressional aspects of culture, Stems as structural, and Roots as foundational aspects of culture.

Learning Intentions
- Recognize and differentiate the multiple levels of culture
- Reflect on personal and professional cultural awareness
- Apply culturally responsive strategies to foster inclusion

Section 2: Exploring the Streams of Engagement

Figure 12: Levels of Culture

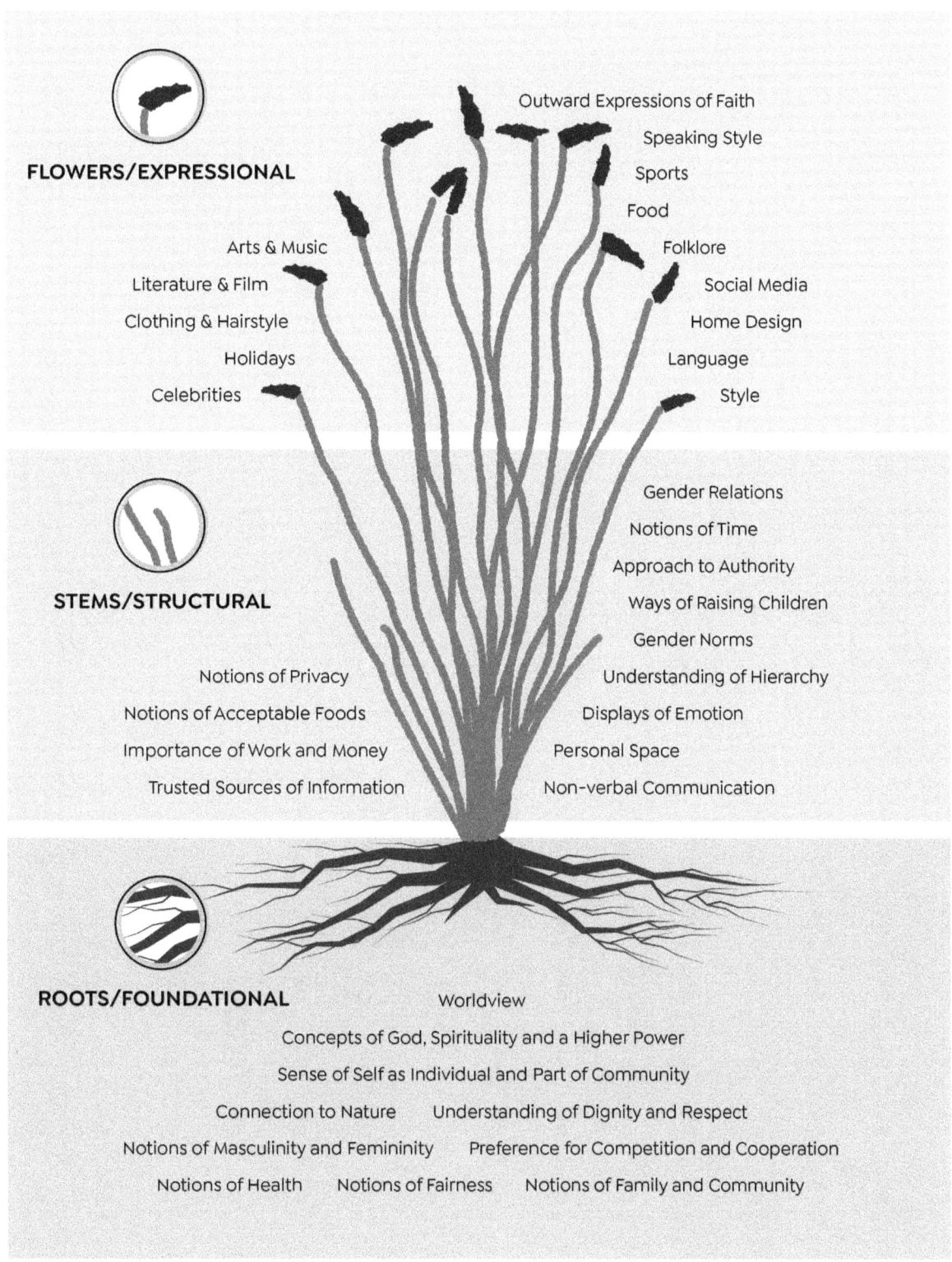

Source: Adapted from Zarette Hammond, 2014.

Round One: Understanding the Multiple Levels of Culture

Choose a partner. Discuss the different aspects of culture as indicated by Flowers, Stems, and Roots. Brainstorm as many characteristics in each category as you can and write them below. There are many aspects of culture that may live in all three levels, like hairstyle.

Flowers/ Expressional
visible and audible aspects of culture we choose to express
Example: *I wear my hair in braids.*
Stems/ Structural
aspects of culture that give shape, complexity, and organization to our shared experience
Example: *My hair represents my ethnic culture, our history, and my style.*
Roots/ Foundational
aspects of culture that provide the bedrock of our spirituality and worldview
Example: *My hair is my power. Please don't ask to touch it.*

Round Two: Small Group Discussion
- Is there a level that is more important than the others?
- Which level do people need to know you to really know what is important to you?
- What level of culture are others often judged?
- What level of culture do most conflicts occur?

Round Three: Individual Reflection
Reflect on your perceptions of a specific group of students. Identify where your practice aligns—at the *flower, stem, and root* level—and recognize areas for growth.
1. Flower Aspects of Culture - *The most tangible and visible aspects and audible of culture, including material expressions of culture such as food, clothing, music, artifacts, and celebrations.*

Indicators:
- I recognize and acknowledge my students' visible cultural traits (e.g., clothing, food, holidays, artifacts, music).
- I include students' cultural expressions (e.g., traditional attire, foods, festivals, art forms) in classroom discussions or celebrations.
- I display multicultural books, posters, or learning materials that reflect students' backgrounds.
- I am aware of the languages spoken by my students and make efforts to pronounce their names correctly.

Reflection: Do I mostly acknowledge culture at the material level, or do I seek a deeper understanding of its meaning?
2. Stem Aspects of Culture - *This level involves behavioral cultural values, social roles, language, communication styles, and how culture shapes behaviors and interactions.*

Indicators:
- I recognize that cultural values (e.g., collectivism versus individualism, communication norms, respect for authority) shape students' participation in learning.
- I adjust my instructional approaches to support different cultural learning preferences (e.g., storytelling, oral traditions, group collaboration).
- I reflect on how my cultural background and biases influence my expectations for students.
- I engage with families and communities to better understand students' lived experiences and learning needs.

- I validate and respect students' ways of communicating, including nonverbal cues, silence, or indirect responses.

Reflection: How often do I examine my own assumptions and adapt my teaching to honor students' cultural ways of being?

3. Roots Aspects of Culture - *At the deepest level, involving values, beliefs, customs, spirituality, and ways of knowing that shape identity and worldviews.*

Indicators:

- I integrate students' cultural identities, lived experiences, and funds of knowledge into the curriculum.
- I create opportunities for students to explore and express their cultural identities through storytelling, projects, or discussions.
- I engage in ongoing professional learning to deepen my understanding of cultural identity, systemic inequities, and their impact on learning.
- I advocate for systemic changes in my school or district that affirm and uplift diverse cultural identities.
- I challenge deficit narratives by using asset-based language and designing inclusive learning experiences.

Reflection: How do I ensure that my understanding of culture moves beyond recognition toward meaningful instructional change?

Personal Reflection

Know Self
- What level of your culture do you share at school?

Know Students
- At what levels of culture do you get to know your students?

Know Practice
- When looking at the different levels of culture, do you elevate one more than the others in your teaching?

Definition of Cultural Competence

Description

As mentioned in our discussion of the *Achievement Triangle*, the work to become a culturally responsive educator requires us to examine ourselves, seek to understand our students, and grow our practice in ways that support student success: know self, know students, and know practice. Used as a conceptual framework for the Stewardship process at a personal and professional level, the *Achievement Triangle* reflects a growth mindset pathway toward cultural competence. As our students change, so should our knowledge and skills evolve to respond to who students are today.

Cultural competency has been extensively researched over the last several decades (Betancourt et al., 2003; Cormier, 2020; Garneau & Pepin, 2014) and is broadly linked to our ability to understand, appreciate, and interact with people from cultures or belief systems different from one's own. When we assume this only applies to our instructional practices, some may focus solely on how they teach rather than the necessity to examine self. Self-understanding is the bridge to understanding our students, their families, and our communities in the interest of promoting equity and excellence.

This engagement is about personal reflection on the term *cultural competence*. It is an opportunity to discuss this concept that will guide your personal and professional growth throughout the Stewardship process. Grounding your work in this deeper understanding of cultural competence can guide all of your actions going forward.

Learning Intentions

- Provide a functional definition of cultural competence
- Cultivate an understanding of why examining one's own culture, beliefs, and assumptions is a prerequisite to forming effective relationships with those who don't share our culture or perspective

Cultural Competence is:

Having the courage, humility, and grace to critically examine one's own assumptions and cultural conditioning, while demonstrating the will and the ability to form authentic and effective relationships across the broad range of intersectional differences.

Use the Frayer Model below to unpack the meaning of cultural competence and to reflect on how cultural competence is showing up in your school.

Cultural Competence Frayer Model

Definition *Create a paraphrased version of the definition by underlining key words and identifying synonyms.*	**Characteristics** *List qualities or traits of cultural competence.*
Example *Identify one example of how cultural competence shows up in your school.*	**Non-Example** *Identify one non-example as an instance where it is missing in your school.*

Personal Reflection

Address each of the following questions to gauge where you are in relation to the goal of becoming more culturally competent:

Know Self

- What are the assumptions or cultural conditioning you've been most challenged to examine?

- What does courage look like for you in engaging across differences?

- How has your own cultural background shaped your sense of identity in professional settings?

Know Students

- How does cultural competence—or the lack of it—affect your relationships with students?

- What feedback have students or families shared that informs your growth in this area?

- How do your students' cultural expressions challenge or expand your worldview?

Know Practice

- How do you assess and grow your cultural competence in your current role?

- What systems or supports exist in your school to build collective cultural competence?

- Where could you strengthen your instructional or relational practices through deeper cultural understanding?

¿Quiénes Somos? (Who Are We?)

Description

This engagement strategy is designed to personalize the concept of cultural competence and connect it to what it means to be an "Empowered Steward." Cultural competence was defined in the previous engagement as:

Having the courage, humility, and grace to critically examine one's own assumptions and cultural conditioning, while demonstrating the will and the ability to form authentic and effective relationships across the broad range of intersectional differences.

In this activity, participants reflect on someone from their own life who has served as a role model in building authentic and respectful relationships across differences. These individuals, whom we call Empowered Steward role models, embody the personal qualities and behaviors central to the work of equity and belonging.

Through one-on-one interviews, participants will share stories about their role models, listen deeply to one another, and collaboratively identify a list of key Empowered Steward qualities. This collective wisdom will be captured and shared after the session, serving as an important touchstone for future engagements, including *Personal Growth Projects* (Stream 2) and *The Seven Commitments of Stewardship* (Stream 4).

Learning Intentions

- Personalize the concept of cultural competence by sharing stories of our Empowered Steward role models
- Strengthen relationships among participants
- Identify Empowered Steward behaviors and qualities
- Encourage participants to consider how they could grow their own capacities for building authentic relationships across differences

Section 2: Exploring the Streams of Engagement

¿Quiénes Somos? (Who Are We?)

Choose a partner and interview them with the following questions:
- Who is an Empowered Steward role model for you—someone who has the courage to question their own assumptions and who knows how to be respectful and inclusive with people from a broad range of different cultures, identities, and backgrounds?

- What personal qualities and behaviors are demonstrated by your role model?

Remember your partner's responses to these questions and ask permission to share them in your discussion group.

Personal Reflection

Know Self
- What were your thoughts and feelings as you considered who has been your Empowered Steward role model?

- What came up for you as you shared the story of your role model with your interview partner and as they shared theirs with you?

- In what ways and with whom do you think you may be serving as an Empowered Steward role model?

- If it is doable, will you share this experience with the person you chose as your role model?

Know Students
- How can learning about others' role models help you better understand and connect with your students?

- What Empowered Steward behaviors might help you create more inclusive learning environments?

- How might your students also serve as role models in building authentic relationships?

Know Practice
- What small steps can you take to intentionally strengthen your Empowered Steward capacities?

- How can you weave Empowered Steward behaviors into your daily practices with students and colleagues?

- In what ways can you celebrate and model authentic engagement across diverse identities in your work?

Lenses of Difference

"Knowing yourself is the beginning of all wisdom."

– Aristotle

Description

The definition of *cultural competence* used throughout this guidebook is about having the courage to know yourself better, the willingness to examine your own assumptions, and the capacity to cultivate authentic relationships across different identities. Those different lenses shape how we experience the world. As stewards of educational ecosystems, cultural competence is central to our effectiveness as professionals. This engagement helps us identify the multiple ways our cultural and linguistic group memberships align with those of our students. The multiple groups to which we belong—these *lenses of difference*—impact who we are and how we show up, both personally and professionally. The same is true for our students and the multiple lenses they bring to the classroom. When we can name our lenses and those of our students, we can better examine what skills and abilities we currently have to cultivate relationships, the precursor to learning.

The ADDRESSING model, developed by Pamela Hays (2016), was initially designed for psychological and multicultural counseling contexts, but can also be applied in education. Using this framework provides a structured way for educators to reflect on and examine the many facets of their own identities. This self-reflection supports continuous personal growth and enhances interactions with diverse students. When educators are explicit about their own identities, they are better equipped to affirm and recognize their students' diverse backgrounds, such as age, ability, ethnicity, and more. This process helps prevent the invisibility and marginalization that occur when unique perspectives are overlooked – and it helps foster trust, belonging, and increased engagement in the classroom (Hays, 2016; Wadsworth et al., 2016). Ultimately, being attentive to both our own and our students' identities equips us to address inequities and advocate for a more just and inclusive learning environment.

Regularly engaging in structured self-reflection using the prompts below can be a powerful first step toward understanding and navigating cultural connections and mismatches in educational settings. By revisiting these prompts over time, educators can deepen their awareness of how their own and others' identities shape classroom dynamics, relationships, and learning experiences.

Learning Intentions

Recognize that everyone in the school community—both students and staff—brings multiple dimensions of identity to our shared environment.

- Identify and name the various identities present within ourselves and throughout our school ecosystem.
- Explore how our different identities intersect, shaping our experiences and perspectives.

Use the table below to guide your reflections. In each row:

1. Reflect on how you personally identify within each lens.
2. Consider the identities of your students (this could be your entire class, a group, or a specific student).
3. Reflect on a colleague and note the identities they represent in each lens.
4. Identify any additional lenses you believe are important but not listed.

The ADDRESSING Framework (Adapted for Educator Reflection)

Lenses	Your Lenses	Lenses of Students (choose a group or individual)	Lenses of Your Colleague[1] (choose one)
Age & Generational			
Disability			
Religion			
Ethnicity			
Social Class			
Sexual Orientation			
Indigenous Membership			
Nationality			
Gender			
Gender Identity			
Language			
What lenses are missing?			

Source: Adapted from Hays, 2008.

Personal Reflection

Know Self

- Which of your lenses do you think about the most?

- Which of your lenses do you think your students see first? Last?

- Where do you notice the greatest differences or mismatches between your own lenses and those of your students (or a specific student/colleague)? How have these differences influenced your interactions, positively or negatively?

Know Students

- What lenses of difference do you have in common with your students?

- What lenses of your students do you know the most about? The least?

Know Practice

- How does power shift based on the differences in these lenses?

- How might these lenses of difference reduce your effectiveness with your students?

- What are ways you do now or can begin to connect with your students by affirming their different lenses?

Scan the QR code to visit our additional resources that support the understanding of how our lenses of difference are impacted by power and privilege.

Identity Triangle

"Knowing yourself is the beginning of all wisdom."

– Aristotle

Description

This engagement strategy invites participants to use the Identity Triangle as a reflective tool for exploring how assigned, claimed, and affinity identities shape their experiences. As Empowered Stewards, developing cultural competence begins with knowing ourselves and recognizing the interplay of individuality, group membership, and shared humanity.

Through structured prompts and small-group dialogue, participants map their own identity triangles and consider how these layers influence their beliefs, behaviors, and relationships. This activity surfaces both the visible and invisible aspects of identity and creates space to recognize how identity evolves over time and across contexts. The reflections generated here deepen empathy and prepare participants for the next engagement, *Culture Toss*, where identity is explored interpersonally through stories and artifacts.

Learning Intentions

- Reflect how assigned, claimed, and affinity identities shape our experiences and perspectives.
- Strengthen self-awareness as a foundation for interpersonal and systemic change.
- Build readiness to engage in identity-centered dialogue and inclusive community practices.

Understanding the Identity Triangle

The Identity Triangle is a tool for personal reflection that supports educators and leaders in exploring the complex layers of their identities. Developed by the Reach Center, the Identity Triangle offers a holistic framework for understanding ourselves as individuals, group members, and participants in shared humanity (Howard, 2006). It invites us to reflect on three key facets:

- **Assigned identities** are how others perceive or label us based on visible or assumed characteristics (e.g., race, gender, language).

- **Claimed identities** are how we define ourselves based on lived experience, belief, or choice (e.g., artist, advocate, survivor).
- **Affinity identities** are how we connect with others through shared experiences, roles, or interests (e.g., teachers, parents, caretakers).

Each of these categories contributes to our sense of self and shapes how we engage with others. The power of the Identity Triangle lies in its recognition that identity is dynamic and intersecting, not fixed or one-dimensional. It helps us recognize that we carry multiple truths at once: we are uniquely ourselves, shaped by our group affiliations, and united by our common humanity.

This model cautions against overemphasizing any one dimension. Prioritizing individuality may obscure the privileges or social structures that benefit us. Focusing solely on group identity may reinforce stereotypes or limit personal nuance. And centering only shared humanity risks erasing the cultural, racial, and social differences that deeply influence experience.

By surfacing and mapping our identities, we strengthen our self-awareness, build empathy, and develop the reflective capacity that is foundational to cultural competence. This self-exploration lays the groundwork for deeper engagement with others and directly supports the next strategy, *Culture Toss*, where these insights are shared and honored in community.

Figure 13: Identity Triangle

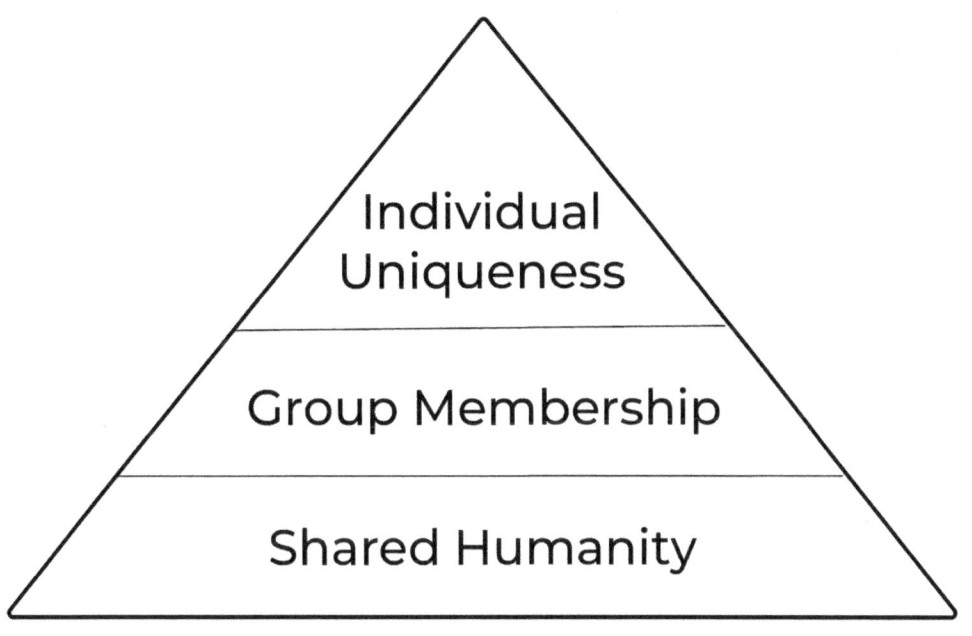

Source: *Adapted from Joe Boyer – Used with Permission*

Use your understanding of the Identity Triangle (figure 13) to reflect on your identity as a unique individual, a member of certain groups, and a member of the larger human community.

Identity Triangle Template

Unique Individual Name some individual aspects about you.

Member of Groups Name a few lenses of difference to which you belong.

Shared Humanity Identify a few experiences shared by all humans.

Personal Reflection

Know Self
- What are some of your most salient claimed, assigned, and affinity identities?

- Which aspects of your identity feel most visible to others? Which feel unseen?

Know Students
- How might your students define or experience their claimed, assigned, and affinity identities?

- In what ways can understanding identity categories help you respond to students with greater empathy?

Know Practice
- How might mapping your own identity using the triangle shape your approach to relationship-building?

- How could you incorporate identity reflection into classroom routines or community-building activities?

Culture Toss

"To be yourself in a world that is constantly trying to make you something else is the greatest accomplishment."

– Ralph Waldo Emerson

Description

This engagement strategy sets the foundation for many conversations to come. It allows the adults in your school to experience how each of us carries our multiple identities at the same time, and the powerful ways that school culture can either support or diminish our intersecting cultural identities or our "personal culture." For some, the idea that our identities impact how we are perceived and treated by others may be new. This simulation is designed to shed light on the factors that might be causing both adults and students to bring less than their full energy to the teaching and learning process; by increasing our awareness of how we and our students experience the culture of our schools, this engagement also enhances our understanding of the barriers that stand in the way of teams achieving their desired outcomes. Make sure you allow ample time for reflection and debriefing during and after this engagement strategy. The lessons of *Culture Toss* come not only from the activity itself but also from the conversations that continue afterward.

The *Culture Toss* engagement asks that we put ourselves in the situation of naming things important to us and imagining what happens when we have them taken away. The Identity Triangle concepts from the previous engagement strategy (shown in Figure 13) support our understanding of culture. Each aspect contributes to our overall identity, but an overemphasis on any single facet can lead to problematic perspectives. By acknowledging our individuality, group affiliations, and common humanity, we can better appreciate the rich tapestry of our experience as humans and foster more empathetic and inclusive spaces.

Learning Intentions

- Provide an experiential understanding of personal culture
- Create awareness of the ways that power, privilege, and oppression can impact personal identity

- Demonstrate the concepts of "negotiating identity" and "intersectionality"
- Reflect on the ways that school culture can cause some students to not bring their whole selves to the classroom

Facilitation Notes

Engage with the Identity Triangle reflection before the Culture Toss. This helps everyone anchor what they choose to share in a broader understanding of their intersecting identities.

Step 1:
- Fill in each box with something meaningful or important to you in that category. Think back to the Identity Triangle as you make your decisions.
- Be honest, but only share what you feel comfortable naming.

Culture Toss Activity Template

Race/Ethnicity	Religion/Spirituality
Language	Life Value
Vocation	Possession

Visit the Stream 2 Resources on our website for a Culture Toss Activity example.

The First Toss:
- Review your completed template.
- Now imagine entering a new school, team, or workplace where fitting in feels important.
- Cross off *two boxes* that you think you'd have to give up, hide, or downplay in order to feel accepted.
- Pause to reflect on what that feels like.

Small Group Conversation after the First Toss:
- Which two boxes did you cross off and why?

The Second Toss:
- Now imagine the stakes are even higher—perhaps the need to be accepted, safe, or successful is even more intense.
- Cross off *two more boxes*, leaving only two remaining.
- Pause again and think about what you chose to hold onto.

Small Group Conversation after the Second Toss:
- Which two boxes did you cross off this time?

- Why did you keep the two boxes that are left?

Application

- How do you see the members of our school community experiencing pressure to give up aspects of their own identities or not be fully who they are?

- Which identities are being targeted the most?

  ⇨ What systems are present or need to be created that address this?

- In what ways are the adults in your school creating this pressure for students not to be who they are?

  ⇨ What is needed to support the adults in growing their cultural competence?

Personal Reflection

Know Self

- What did you choose to bring to the Culture Toss and why?

- What aspects of your identity have you felt pressure to hide or leave behind?

Know Students

- What might your students bring to the classroom that isn't always seen or valued?

- How can you help students feel safe bringing their full selves into learning spaces?

Know Practice

- What conditions help create a space where everyone feels safe to share who they are?

- How might you adapt the Culture Toss in your classroom or with your team to build belonging?

Stereotype Threat Research

Description

Stereotype threat is a concept in social psychology that refers to the phenomenon wherein individuals experience anxiety or concern about confirming negative stereotypes related to their identity group. This anxiety can impact performance and behavior in situations where the stereotype is relevant. The concept was first introduced and extensively studied by Claude Steele and Joshua Aronson in the 1990s.

As stereotype threat research has demonstrated, the interpersonal and cultural context of learning has a profound impact on students' motivation and performance. Suppose students feel a lack of belonging, a low level of trust in the people around them, or a sense that teachers do not value their intelligence. In that case, their feelings of competence, their motivation, and their performance will be lessened (Steele & Aronson, 2005).

Since then, numerous studies and articles have been published exploring stereotype threat and its implications (Pennington et al., 2016; Walton & Spencer, 2009).

This activity allows us to reflect on the students we currently serve and engage in conversations with team members about how we see stereotype threat evidenced in their experiences, specifically those groups identified in your *School Outcomes Assessment* discussion as "missing or not engaging." Stereotype threat is one way that internalized oppression becomes activated. Students are aware of the ways that externally imposed stereotypes target them, and that sense of threat diminishes their self-image and their efficacy in the world, specifically in the classroom. Grounding our work in an understanding of stereotype threat supports us all in growing our knowledge and skills with others and activating a growth mindset. Addressing and challenging educational inequities requires comprehensive efforts to dismantle stereotypes, combat prejudice, eliminate discriminatory practices, and promote social justice and equity for all individuals in our school communities.

Description

Learning Intentions

- Identify ways in which societal realities of prejudice and stereotypes impact student outcomes
- Introduce the concept of stereotype threat
- Make a connection between stereotype threat and the student outcomes you have observed in your classroom/school
- Consider how you and your colleagues can reduce the impact of stereotype threat for those students you have acknowledged you are missing or not engaging

Reflective Small Group Discussion

- Think together about the statement:

    If students feel a lack of belonging or a low level of trust in the people around them, or a sense that teachers do not value their intelligence, then their feelings of competence, their motivation, and their performance will be lessened (Aronson & Steele, 2005).

- What evidence do you see that these elements of stereotype threat are impacting the group of students your team identified in the *School Outcomes Assessment*?

- Are there ways that the actions and views of adults in your school/district may be contributing to the presence of stereotype threat for the students who are disengaged in school?

- What are ways your students may be experiencing stereotype threat in their neighborhoods and the broader community?

- What are some ways you could lessen the impact of stereotype threat for your students?

- What are the ways these dynamics might be showing up for your colleagues? What is your role?

Personal Reflection

Know Self
- How have stereotypes about your identities impacted you?

Know Students
- How have stereotypes about the identities of your students impacted them?

Know Practice
- In what ways might you be contributing to the stereotype threat your students are experiencing?

- Can you identify ways you could counter the impacts of stereotypes on your students?

Stages of Personal Growth Toward Cultural Competence

"The more you know yourself, the more patience you have for what you see in others."
— Erik Erikson

Description

For this engagement strategy, we once again explore how the *Achievement Triangle* can be a useful model to guide our work as Empowered Stewards. That side of the triangle related to Knowing Self is a consistent theme found in research around becoming a more culturally competent educator. The Stewardship process defines cultural competence as:

Having the courage, humility, and grace to critically examine one's own assumptions and cultural conditioning, while demonstrating the will and the ability to form authentic and effective relationships across the broad range of intersectional differences.

Research supports the idea that self-awareness is linked to greater empathy and understanding of others. A study by Jordan et al. (2019) found that individuals who had a clearer sense of their own identities were more likely to demonstrate empathy toward people from different racial or cultural backgrounds. As educators, we are always working with people who come from lenses of difference other than our own, so a path toward greater understanding of ourselves and others is critical. Many theorists have examined the pathways of personal development toward understanding one's own identity (Cardwell et al., 2020; Carter, 1995; Helms,1994; Howard, 2016; Tatum, 1992; Utt & Tochluk, 2020). Each of these scholars has provided models to support how we learn about self and our own identities in relation to others.

As we have explored earlier in *Stages of Organizational Growth*, the Stewardship work is very much grounded in developmental processes and invariably focuses on growth and improvement. In this engagement, *Stages of Personal Growth Toward Cultural Competence*, the developmental concept of "personal journey" (rooted in the research base cited above) is made explicit. In this engagement, that theoretical work is personalized as you and your colleagues explore the significant passages and personal transformations that each of us experiences on our journey toward greater cultural competence (see Figure 14). Here again, cultural competence is understood not as a destination but as a lifelong process of learning. Participants are invited to share stories related to their identities at various stages in their own lives. What often emerges from these stories is the realization that teaching in a diverse school is in itself a significant catalyst for the personal transformation of many educators, challenging us to rethink old paradigms and belief systems. Cultural competence is not something we either have or don't have; it is acquired and sustained through a lifelong learning process that never ends. As most educators know, and neuroscientific evidence confirms, our brains have a remarkable ability to change and adapt throughout life. As educators, we have the privilege to witness this phenomenon on a day-to-day basis as we experience our students forming new connections, developing and perfecting new skills, and engaging in higher levels of abstract reasoning. This ability to rewire our brain's circuitry is called *neuroplasticity*, and the good news is that it stays with us across our lifespan (Park & Huang, 2010). For these reasons, it might help to think of developing enhanced levels of cultural competence as a reflection of neuroplasticity—a process of *becoming*. With that said, this rewiring isn't necessarily voluntary. Humans have a multitude of experiences, most of which we aren't even consciously aware of. Our brain's ability to filter these experiences helps us to survive. Author Zaretta Hammond reminds us that when a child experiences an "amygdala hijack" as a consequence of negative stimuli (e.g., fear of physical harm), they are in no condition to focus on learning the quadratic equation (Hammond, 2014)! Similarly, becoming culturally competent is also a matter of consciousness and choice, a choice to critically reflect on our own experiences and reactions, a choice to pay attention.

Learning Intentions

- Increase self-awareness through the exploration of identity development models
- Realize how identity is multifaceted and influenced by many factors
- Identify areas for self-improvement and setting goals to become more authentic and fulfilled versions of ourselves, informed by our understanding of identity formation processes

Figure 14: Stages of Personal Growth Toward Cultural Competence

No Interaction	Direct Interaction	Disintegration/ Meltdown	Reintegration	Pseudo Independence	Immersion/ Emersion	Autonomy

Source: Adapted from *Black and White Racial Identity: Theory, Research and Practice*, by J. E. Helms (Greenwood Press, 1990). For further discussion of these stages, see Chapter 5 of *We Can't Teach What We Don't Know* (3rd ed.), by Gary R. Howard (Teachers College Press, 2016).

Stages of Personal Growth Toward Cultural Competence
Note-Taking Chart

⊘	No Interaction	
⊡	Direct Interaction	
◌	Disintegration/Meltdown	
→⊡	Reintegration	
⊙	Pseudo Independence	
◎	Immersion/Emersion	
☀	Autonomy	

Source: Adapted from *Black and White Racial Identity: Theory, Research and Practice*, by J. E. Helms (Greenwood Press, 1990). For further discussion of these stages, see Chapter 5 of *We Can't Teach What We Don't Know* (3rd ed.), by Gary R. Howard (Teachers College Press, 2016).

Visit the Stream 2 Resources on our website for a completed examples of the Stages of Personal Growth Toward Cultural Competence

	Stages of Personal Growth Toward Cultural Competence
	Example: Teacher raised in home with Catholic faith begins working with many Muslim faith students and families.
⊘	**No Interaction** • Believes one's own cultural values and faith are the "norm." • Has little or no exposure to people of Muslim faith outside of stereotypes in media. • Makes decisions and forms opinions based solely on one's own monocultural experiences.
⊡	**Direct Interaction** • Begins interacting with Muslim students and their families in the classroom. • Observes cultural and religious practices for the first time outside media depictions. • Experiences initial discomfort, uncertainty, or fear based on previously internalized messages and biases. • Initiates basic communication and practical collaboration.
(tilted ⊡)	**Disintegration/Meltdown** • Develops a genuine connection (e.g., through a parent volunteer or classroom event) with a Muslim individual. • Feels internal conflict between pre-existing beliefs about Muslims and positive interactions. • Begins questioning media-fueled narratives amid real-life experiences. • Experiences emotional discomfort or guilt over previous assumptions.
•⇥	**Reintegration** • Encounters external pressures (e.g., family or news events) that reinforce prior fears and biases. • Feels torn between evolving personal experience and loyalty to one's cultural group. • May withdraw from new intercultural relationships due to confusion or discomfort. • Seeks support or validation from one's original cultural circle.
⊙	**Pseudo Independence** • Begins to intellectually accept the possibility of broader worldviews. • May seek information about Islam and Muslim culture from books, documentaries, or reputable sources. • Shows empathy and respect for differences, but relates to these primarily at a "safe" distance. • Support for diversity is more intellectual/abstract than personal or emotional.

Source: Adapted from *Black and White Racial Identity: Theory, Research and Practice*, by J. E. Helms (Greenwood Press, 1990). For further discussion of these stages, see Chapter 5 of *We Can't Teach What We Don't Know* (3rd ed.), by Gary R. Howard (Teachers College Press, 2016).

Section 2: Exploring the Streams of Engagement

Stages of Personal Growth Toward Cultural Competence
Example: Teacher raised in home with Catholic faith begins working with many Muslim faith students and families.

	Immersion/Emersion • Deeply explores and reflects on personal beliefs and cultural identity. • Actively engages in intercultural dialogue, genuinely seeking to understand others' points of view. • Challenges and reconstructs old stereotypes and fosters new, inclusive attitudes. • Feels empowered by relationships across cultural boundaries; personal growth is evident through new behaviors.
	Autonomy • Comfortably interact and build relationships across cultural, racial, or religious boundaries without anxiety or defensiveness. • Take initiative for ongoing growth, seeking feedback, continued learning, and direct engagement with others different from themselves. • Integrate knowledge of cultural diversity into all aspects of work and life, including policies, practices, and interpersonal relationships. • Consistently recognize, challenge, and interrupt bias or discrimination, both personally and systemically, in everyday situations.

Source: Adapted from *Black and White Racial Identity: Theory, Research and Practice*, by J. E. Helms (Greenwood Press, 1990). For further discussion of these stages, see Chapter 5 of *We Can't Teach What We Don't Know* (3rd ed.), by Gary R. Howard (Teachers College Press, 2016).

Small Group Conversation

1. Share a story about your personal experience with one or more of these stages connected to the focus group from the *School Outcomes Assessment*.

2. How might the stage you are in with the focus group inform/influence/motivate the work you do, how you do it, and why you do it?

3. How can we support ourselves, our colleagues, our students, and our school community in better navigating the journey through the stages of cultural competence?

4. Are these stages experienced differently by people of color as compared to White people? By gender-fluid people as compared to those who firmly uphold the existence of the gender binary and identify as either male or female? By recent immigrants? By other diversities as compared to dominant culture identities?

Personal Reflection

Know Self

- Related to the student identity group you focused on, which stage of growth toward cultural competence are you currently in?

- What experiences or relationships have most influenced your growth with this specific group?

- What internal challenges might you encounter as you continue to grow?

Know Students

- How do you see your students navigating different stages of development related to cultural competence?

- How can recognizing these stages help you support students' social-emotional and academic growth?

- How might your own experiences with growth influence the way you understand students' needs and experiences?

Know Practice

- How can you design classroom experiences that foster growth in cultural competence for yourself and your students?

- What routines or practices could you build into your teaching to encourage critical self-reflection?

- How might you use your understanding of identity development to create more inclusive and affirming learning environments?

Personal Growth Project

Description

As the *Achievement Triangle* illustrates, the journey toward developing our ability to be culturally responsive requires work at both the personal and professional levels. The *Personal Growth Project* is a culminating activity for Stream 2 and connects to several engagement activities throughout the Stewardship process. Each member of your team will design and commit to carrying out a personalized action growth project that will expand their capacity for cultural competence, which we have defined as Your Stewardship facilitators will share stories of their own experience with each of these stages. Use this note-taking sheet to record what you are learning about each stage, and reflect on your own journey through the process.

This engagement will focus on one of the student identity groups you elevated in the *School Outcomes Assessment* for whom you and your colleagues are "missing the mark or not engaging." The Personal Growth Project asks that we do an inquiry into knowing ourselves regarding this specific identity group, and improving our practice. This project is about gaining more self-knowledge by critically examining where our assumptions and cultural conditioning could be getting in the way. This act of self-inquiry supports a deeper understanding of our impact and provides opportunities for us to expand our capacity to create inclusive learning environments for all students. This activity is best done at the same time, or closely following, the work with the *Stages of Organizational Growth*. As a team, identify the length of the project and how projects will be shared.

Learning Intentions

- Engage individuals in deepening their practice as cultural stewards
- Identify personal goals for growing their capacity for cultural competence
- Design personalized action projects that further goals for growing cultural competence
- Connect this project to one of the focus group you identified in your *School Outcomes Assessment*

Planning Your Personal Growth Project

For our purposes, cultural competence is defined as *Having the courage, humility, and the grace to critically examine one's own assumptions and cultural conditioning, while demonstrating the will and the ability to form authentic and effective relationships across the broad range of intersectional differences.*

Goal: I will work toward growing my cultural competence related to: _____.

(Focus Group from School Outcomes Assessment [S1])

Step One: Initial Personal Reflection:

Based on your stage, you identified in *Stages of Growth Towards Cultural Competence* regarding your team's focus group of students, go deeper with the reflection questions below.

No Interaction	Direct Interaction	Disintegration/ Meltdown	Reintegration	Pseudo Independence	Immersion/ Emersion	Autonomy

Source: Adapted from *Black and White Racial Identity: Theory, Research and Practice*, by J. E. Helms (Greenwood Press, 1990). For further discussion of these stages, see Chapter 5 of *We Can't Teach What We Don't Know* (2nd ed.), by Gary R. Howard (Teachers College Press, 2006).

- What are a few messages I got about this group as a child?
- What life experiences do I have with this group of students?
    - ⇨ Personal
    - ⇨ Professional
- Have the experiences I've had with this group been primarily positive or negative?
    - ⇨ Personal
    - ⇨ Professional
- What have been some of the factors that have contributed to these experiences?
- What messages in mainstream media taught me about this group?

- How have these messages and experiences influenced my behaviors toward this group?
  ⇨ Personal
  ⇨ Professional
- What is my current level of comfort with students in this focus group?

Step Two: Action Steps

Identify actions you will take to grow your capacity to foster authentic relationships with this group of students. Reflect on whether this project pushes you to learn at a surface, shallow, or deep level regarding this group.

Record your action steps here:

Action Step:	
Action Step:	
Action Step:	

For more examples, follow the QR code to the online resources. Look for Stream 2 and then Personal Project Growth Project.

Step Three: Assessment

How will you assess the impact of the Personal Growth Project in a way that includes student voice? Establish a timeline for your project.

Action Step	Assessment/Monitoring	Deadline & Benchmark Dates

Step Four: Allies and Critical Friends

Identify the people who can help you accomplish your goal and reflect on your progress.

Step Five: Concluding Personal Reflection

Know Self

- After working on my Personal Growth Project, what is my current level of comfort with students in this focus group?

Know Students

- What new connections and relationships have formed as a result of my Personal Growth Project?

Know Practice

- How has my Personal Growth Project impacted my practice related to students in this focus group?

In My One Beat

This is a creative expression engagement designed to explore the complex and multidimensional nature of identity. The *In My One Beat* poem template (Figure 15) is an opportunity to explore self, our connections across differences, and the possibility of growing a community rooted in care and knowledge. Culture is built on a foundation of shared stories, and the ecosystem of relationships that make a community is built on those same stories. This engagement is an opportunity to fortify that foundation.

Everyone has a unique rhythm, or beat—a way of walking through the world, a way of expressing, a way of being in relationship with others. The *In My One Beat* poem is an invitation to isolate a single beat in time, one beat of the heart—and imagine all that lives in a single moment in the life of a single human being. Your ancestors are there, your passions, your family, your struggle, your traditions, your celebrations, your history, and your hope for the future. This engagement is an opportunity to creatively reflect and grow self-knowledge, to expand your knowledge of people who are different from you through the simple act of listening, to grow your capacity for caring for one another across our differences, and to expand the narrative of who we are as a community.

This engagement strategy was originally adapted from Linda Christensen's "Where I am From" poem structure (Christensen, 2000) It was built out as an experiential engagement by Howard and Born in 2004 and evolved as In My One Beat (Colwell & Howard, 2018)

Learning Intentions

- Bring our personal/cultural stories into the professional learning journey
- Explore the value of personal story in the work of crafting culture/building community.
- Practice and grow care and knowledge—the core aspects of Stewardship

In My One Beat *(sample from a former YES participant)*
In my one beat, I am from platanos and sugar cane in the mountains
Coffee beans roasting in the morning, sandy beaches, and clear paradise
In my one beat I am from freestyle battles in the corners
In my one beat I am alive with double dutch on a warm afternoon.
In my one beat, I taste my mother's rice and beans
The chewy steak on Sunday nights
Yuca and salami when the sun is at its highest
In My One Beat I am filled with the sound of palo drums,
the guitar's song in bachata.
In my one beat is beat boxing and struggle
In my one beat I hear voices of tios and tias,
centuries of Spanish-speaking culture
And endless rivers of family in my one beat.
In my one beat, I am from baggy clothes and shorts
The tambora and guira play in my beat
My one beat is an endless rhythm
Hips that move like the waves of the Caribbean
In my one beat, I am the Dominican Republic
In my one beat, I am New York
In my one beat, I am Karen

Figure 15: In My One Beat Poem

IN MY ONE BEAT

In my one beat ...

In my one beat ...

In my one beat ...

In my one beat ...

In my one beat ...

In my one beat ...

In my one beat ...

In my one beat ...

In my one beat ...

For translated copies of this form, more examples of complete *In My One Beat* poems, and videos of poems being performed, follow the QR code to the online resources. Look for Stream 2 and then In My One Beat.

Personal Reflection

Know Self

- What personal or cultura.. elements came forward most strongly in your beat?

- What have you learned about yourself?

- What surprising knowledge did you gain from the person(s) you shared with and who shared with you?

- What new aspects of your identity might you want to explore further?

Know Students

- How could the *In My One Beat* engagement deepen your understanding of your students' identities?

- In what ways might students benefit from opportunities to tell their own stories?

- How might listening to students' stories shift your teaching or support practices?

Know Practice

- What school spaces might benefit from this engagement?

- What value does this exercise have for growing stewardship?

- What value does this exercise have for growing community?

In My One Beat was developed in collaboration with M. Born and W.A. Colwell

Stream 3: Social Dominance to Justice for All

"The most common way people give up their power is by thinking they don't have any."
— Alice Walker

"We are in the business of cultivating power and renewal. We are growing out of relationships and systems trapped in extractive power dynamics, and we are growing into natural dynamics of generative power."
— Benjie Howard

Stream 3 takes the personal, professional, and organizational conversations you have had up to this point and moves them into the societal, historical, and structural dimensions of the work (see your *Layers of Engagement* notes from Stream 1, Figure 3). If we are to overcome the educational inequities we see manifested in our schools today, we must first sharpen our understanding of the causal factors rooted in our history and still deeply embedded in our schools, communities, and institutional structures. One of the most glaring deficiencies in decades of school reform efforts has been the lack of any political or historical perspective on these causal factors. This deficiency in analysis has given rise to inadequate responses based on the false assumption that we can eliminate educational outcome gaps simply by working within the schools themselves. Related to poverty, for example, a lack of structural analysis has led policymakers to place heavy pressure for testing and accountability on educators working with students in high-poverty schools; however, these same policymakers do essentially nothing to address the causal factors leading to the growing incidence of childhood poverty in the United States (Gorski, 2017). Likewise, related to race, the lack of adequate historical knowledge and the ignoring and disregard of the role of racism in determining housing and school assignment patterns, led the Roberts's Supreme Court to deny school districts the right to use race as a means of overcoming segregation of our nation's schools (*Parents Involved in Community Schools v. Seattle School District No.1*, June 28, 2007). In a similar display of historical ignorance, the court's decision to end affirmative action in higher education admissions policies was based on what Justice Ketanji Brown Jackson described in her dissenting opinion as "a let-them-eat-cake obliviousness" on the part of her fellow Justices (*Students for Fair Admissions v. President and Fellows of Harvard College*, June 29, 2023). Throughout much of our history, this kind of shallow understanding and inadequate structural analysis has led to inadequate policies and legal decisions. This "consciousness gap" is as damaging as the so-called achievement gap—in fact, it is a major cause of it. Educational historian Diane Ravitch provides exhaustive documentation of this lack of informed analysis in her critique of the top-down, market-driven approach to public school reform and concludes:

> The reformers say they care about poverty, but they do not address it other than to insist on private management of the schools in urban districts; the reformers ignore racial segregation altogether, apparently accepting it as inevitable. Thus, they leave the root causes of low academic performance undisturbed. (Ravitch, 2013, p. 6)

Without dismantling our continuing history of dis-consciousness in the statehouse, we can never achieve equity and justice in the schoolhouse. Ravitch's conclusions have continued to be reinforced and are emphasized by Black, Indigenous, and People of Color (BIPOC) researchers Bettina Love (2023) and Shawn Ginwright (2019). Ginwright and Seigel write:

> To place race at the center of conversations and strategies that aim for diversity, equity, and inclusion means moving beyond solving surface problems and acknowledging where and how inequity is baked into current systems and structures. (2019, para. 5)

By focusing on the societal and structural forces that have created and sustained educational inequities, the intent of Stream 3 is neither to overwhelm your faculty and staff with the heaviness of our historical burden nor to give them an excuse to explain away the inequities they see in their own classrooms. The intent, rather, is to reinforce the vital importance of the work they are doing and ignite their passion for justice for all of your students. Many of your colleagues already embrace this deeper vision and passion for their work. They chose the vocation of teaching precisely because they want to provide their students with the tools to overcome any obstacles that the demographics of birth and the prevalence of oppression have put in their way, and give them the full measure of opportunity for creating a good life. These teachers see their work as intimately connected to social justice and the overturning of centuries of racism, classism, heterosexism, and other dimensions of dominance. For other members of your team, however, who may not have made these deeper connections in their own minds and hearts, the Stream 3 activities and discussions will hopefully encourage them to see their work in a new light and engage their students with fresh energy and perspective.

In addition to its focus on the historical and societal dimensions, Stream 3 also invites you and your colleagues and students to consider how issues of privilege, power, and systemic disempowerment function within the culture of your school, district, and community. This exploration is closely tied to the *School Outcomes Assessment* and *Stages of Organizational Growth* engagement strategies that you first encountered and discussed in Stream 1. Revisiting these conversations while exploring how privilege and power play out in your local contexts can be quite powerful. By broadening the scope of our inquiry from the micro level (personal) to the macro (schools, systems, communities), we can now address some challenging but critical questions, including the following:

1. Which student groups (based on identities such as race, social class, gender identity, sexual orientation, religion, language, and special needs) in your school are more included, involved, recognized, and rewarded?
2. Which groups are less privileged and more marginalized?
3. What policies, practices, and assumptions get in the way of full inclusion and equity, and which programs and approaches are working to break down these patterns of separation and disempowerment?
4. In considering the larger ecosystem that impacts our students, including families and the broader community, how might we work together to strengthen respect across differences?

All of these concerns will be the focus of your Stream 3 collaboration.

Learning Intentions

- Explore issues of privilege, power, and dominance
- Understand the dynamics of dominance as they impact your students and your school culture
- Link issues of dominance and disempowerment to the inequities you see manifested in your school, district, and community
- Collaborate with your students and colleagues in the creation of strategies and action plans for moving from social dominance to justice for all

Overview of Engagement Strategies

Stream 3 engagement strategies equip educators and teams to examine systemic injustice and reimagine equity-centered alternatives. These strategies foster the critical inquiry needed to identify and dismantle exclusionary patterns, interrogate power dynamics, and surface root causes of inequity. They provide structured opportunities to reflect on positionality, shift institutional narratives, and design justice-oriented responses to historical and present-day disparities. Refer to the table below for the Stream 3 strategies that support this work of transformation.

Layers of Engagement

The engagement strategies in Stream 3 ask educators to confront history, power, and privilege in order to reimagine justice-centered schools. On a personal level, educators explore their own identities in the context of systemic inequality and reflect on their positionality within systems of dominance. At the professional level, teams investigate patterns of exclusion and define root causes of inequity through collaborative inquiry. Organizationally, this Stream supports the dismantling of policies and practices that perpetuate injustice, replacing them with equitable structures and shared decision-making. These efforts directly engage with and resist societal and structural inequities, forging new paths toward justice within and beyond the school walls.

Engagements that Support Collaborative Inquiry

The YES Collaborative Inquiry Process supports this critical reflection by offering a structure for teams to notice and disrupt inequitable patterns within their own systems. Through cycles of defining root causes and reframing challenges, educators are equipped to address injustice not as isolated incidents, but as systemic conditions requiring collective reimagination. Stream 3 challenges us to dismantle and disrupt interpersonal and systemic dynamics rooted in dominance, disempowerment, and the erasure of others—and to work toward crafting interpersonal and systemic dynamics rooted in shared power. There are two engagement strategies in particular, as shown in Table 4: Applying the Engagements of Stream 3, which support collaborative inquiry most directly. These are especially helpful for deepening awareness, expanding your understanding of root causes, and exploring new actions and strategies in phases 2, 3, and 4.

Key Engagements in Stream 3:

- **We The People:** An experiential strategy to explore the spectrum of historical perspective across your professional community. (Notice and Disrupt, Empathize)

- **The Dynamics of Social Dominance and Privilege and Power Assessment:** This is an unpacking, through a framework and real lived experiences of adults and students in the community, of how social dominance functions in our relationships, in our systems and in classrooms now and throughout history. An examination of what we are "growing out of." (Notice and Disrupt, Empathize, Ideate)

- **Justice in the Words of Elders:** This offers a historical perspective and a grounding in "what we are growing into." (Define, Ideate, Prototype, Evaluate)

Table 4: Applying the Engagements of Stream 3

Strategy	Collaborative Inquiry	Personal (Individual)	Professional (Team)	Organizational (System)
We, the People / *Nican Tlaca*	•	•		•
Dominance to Justice Word Association				•
Dynamics of Social Dominance	•		•	•
Privilege and Power Assessment	•	•	•	•
Justice in the Words of Elders	•	•		•
In My One Beat – Struggle		•	•	•

We, the People / *Nican Tlaca*

Description

We, the People is an experiential engagement strategy originally designed by Gary Howard during the 1987 Bicentennial of the U.S. Constitutional Convention. The activity is intended to deepen a national dialogue about how far we have come in our efforts to make real the promise of freedom, equality, and justice for all originally set forth in 1787. The engagement has evolved based on feedback from educators and students over the past four decades, and it has expanded to include Indigenous perspectives, which allow for a more nuanced lens with regard to the ideals of freedom, equality, and justice, and a longer historical view with regard to the establishment of democratic governance in the Americas—prior to and after European arrival.

The engagement will surface the wide spectrum of political and historical perspectives that exist in your community. It is not a debate to decide whose perspective is better, but rather it is an opportunity to listen to voices we agree with, voices we disagree with, and allow our own lenses and intelligence to be expanded. The art of listening is hard and has been identified as a key learning takeaway by the many educators and students who have participated in this engagement activity.

The central point of *We, the People* is to demonstrate that the issues of equity and diversity that schools and other organizations are dealing with in the 21st century are directly connected to the arrangements of dominance that were established more than two centuries ago in the founding of the nation. We can have different perspectives with regard to just how these issues manifest, but listening to each other's perspectives challenges us to see more clearly how history is alive in our classrooms today.

Learning Intentions

- Describe the historical roots of educational inequities
- Reflect on how systemic dominance continues to shape schools
- Explore and discuss multiple perspectives and complex truths through an interactive experience
- Explain why strategic initiatives related to race, gender, class, and other differences are critically important in today's schools
- Connect national ideals of freedom and justice to school-based equity work

> "The first principle (of the Haudenosaunee Constitution, est. 1450) is peace. The second principle, equity, justice for the people. And third, the power of good minds, of the collective powers to be of one mind: unity and health."
>
> Oren Lyons, Faith Keeper of the Turtle Clan
> Onondaga Council of Chiefs
>
> (Lyons & Moyers, 1991)

Setup Questions

- Who got to be fully included in the conversation to build a set of community agreements for a new nation in 1787?
- Who was left out? Who were the *Nican Tlaca*—the people here today? (See Stream 2, *Homelands Conversation*.)
- What are some of the ideals put into writing in the Declaration of Independence, the Constitution, the Bill of Rights, and the amendments?

Conversation

From 1787 to the present, how far have we have come in making real the promise of freedom, equality, and justice for *all*?

0   10   20   30   40   50   60   70   80   90   100

- Why did you choose your number?
- What is your evidence?
- Who are you thinking about?

Shift your focus to your school or district. Based on its stated values around inclusion, equity, and excellence, how far has your school or district come in making those ideals real?

Personal Reflection

Know Self
- What perspectives inspired or challenged you during the activity?

- Would you change your number after hearing others' reflections? Why?

Know Team
- What did you notice about where people placed themselves on the scale?

- What did you learn about your team, your district, or your broader community?

Know Practice
- What does this exercise in multiple perspectives teach you about your own practice?

- How might you use it in your teaching and leadership?

Dominance to Justice Word Association

Description
One of the core beliefs we carry in this work is that the solutions to the inequities we experience in our school communities must come from the people most impacted by those inequities. The intelligence and depth of thinking required to define the problems we face, and to imagine the kind of social/professional dynamics we want to create, should also come primarily from the community. The work of Empowered Stewards might best be described as the work of disrupting and dismantling interpersonal and systemic dynamics rooted in social dominance (or power misused in order to disempower others) and working toward or building interpersonal and systemic dynamics rooted in shared power—the difference between power *over* and power *with*. This work can also be described as growing out of extractive power dynamics and into generative power dynamics. The following engagement strategies are designed to draw out the collective wisdom in the community in order to define what we are working to disrupt and what we want to work toward.

When sharing this engagement with middle and high school students, we will often offer back the students' own associations with the concepts of justice and dominance, then give them the *Webster Dictionary* definitions and ask which is the more thorough, complex, and intelligent way of defining the concepts. They will always choose their own collective thinking over the dictionary—an effective way to celebrate their wisdom!

Learning Intentions
- Define dominance and justice using shared community wisdom
- Examine the range of perspectives and experiences within your group
- Lay the groundwork for deeper conversations about power, privilege, and equity

Figure 16: Justice Over Dominance

JUSTICE

dominance

Dominance to Justice Word Association developed in collaboration with M. Born.

Small Group Discussion
- What similarities do you notice with our collective associations with the two concepts?

- What contradictions?

Personal Reflection

Know Self
- What did you learn from the experience of collectively defining these concepts?

- What personal experiences influence your definitions of dominance and justice?

Know Students
- How do you think your students define these terms?

Know Practice
- Write your own definitions of dominance and justice.

How can these definitions inform your work as an Empowered Steward in your school or district?

Dynamics of Social Dominance

Description

If the work of an Empowered Steward is primarily the work of dismantling and disrupting interpersonal and systemic dynamics rooted in social dominance and working to build relational and systemic dynamics rooted in justice and equity, we must first heighten our awareness of how social dominance manifests in both our relationships and our systems. We offer the definition and the dynamics as a starting point to explore how the dynamics are real in our own lives, in our professional experiences, and in the systems we serve.

Learning Intentions

- Build a conceptual framework for understanding issues of social dominance
- Relate the *We, the People* experience to the *Dynamics of Social Dominance*
- Create a systemic foundation for understanding and working with educational inequities
- Explain how dominance operates in relationships and institutions

Definition of Social Dominance (Howard, 2006)

Social dominance is . . .

- Systems of privilege and preference
- Reinforced by power
- Favoring certain groups over others

The Dynamics of Social Dominance		
Luxury of Ignorance	Assumption of Rightness	The Legacy of Privilege
Being unaware of injustice because you are not affected by it	The belief that one person's or group's truth is *the* truth	The historical and ongoing giving of opportunities, resources, and privileges to one group of people and not to others

Small Group Discussion

Know Self

- How have you experienced or benefited from one or more of these dynamics in your life?

Know Students

- How do these dynamics show up in your classroom or school?

- How might they be affecting your students' sense of belonging, safety, or potential?

Know Practice

- What will it take to shift school culture from dominance to justice?

- What is one small but meaningful action you can take to begin that shift?

Privilege and Power Assessment

Description

This engagement strategy asks you, your colleagues, and students to apply the conceptual framework provided in Stream 3 to the realities of your school, district, or community culture. How do systems of power, privilege, and preference impact the lives of students, employees, and families? Which identity groups are empowered and which are disempowered? How does this differential access to power manifest itself in people's experiences within the culture of your school? How do issues of power and privilege undergird the evidence of inequities you see manifested in your school outcomes—inequities related to access to higher-level courses, inclusion in extracurricular activities, lack of access to culturally relevant curriculum and instruction, graduation rates, disproportionate discipline referral rates, enrichment opportunities, attendance, school boundary assignments, differential resourcing of schools, degree of parental engagement, and other dimensions of schooling?

The movement from the realities of dominance to the creation of justice for all depends, first of all, on our recognition and acknowledgment of the ways that power and privilege are functioning to create inequities in the context of our schools, our communities, and our nation as a whole. Systems of privilege and preference thrive in silence and invisibility, where the arrangements of social dominance are ingrained into "business as usual" and function beneath the level of our consciousness. The late David Foster Wallace, an acclaimed novelist and essayist, offered a great metaphor for what we mean by "business as usual." During his commencement address at Kenyon College, he told the story of two young fish, happily swimming, attending to their (fish) business as usual. They encounter an elder fish who greets them with "How's the water, kids?" Shortly thereafter, one of the younger fish looks at the other and asks, "What the hell is water?" In other words, when we live our lives immersed in inequities (the "business as usual"), it can be difficult to fathom that there are even alternatives to them. Stream 3 as a whole, and this *Privilege and Power Assessment*, in particular, are intended to bring the unconscious into consciousness. By closing this consciousness gap, we open the possibility for the healing work to begin. Hopefully, you, along with your colleagues and your students, can enter this conversation in a courageous and authentic way, creating a brave space where together you name that which has been unnamed and move away from the dynamics of "power over" and toward the possibilities of "power with."

It would be helpful to pair this engagement strategy with the work you did previously related to the *School Outcomes Assessment*. When thinking about the groups of students you identified as those "we are missing or not engaging," a deeper understanding and acknowledgment of the realities of power and privilege will often open the door to more specific and effective reparative responses.

Learning Intentions

- Apply the dynamics of dominance discussion to the realities of your school, district, or community
- Identify how "*systems of privilege and preference, reinforced by power, favoring certain groups and disempowering others*" are functioning in your school setting
- Examine the ways in which the dynamics of dominance may be getting in the way of equitable outcomes
- Recognize how the dynamics of dominance intersect with your earlier work with the *School Outcomes Assessment*
- Design strategies for reducing the impact of privilege and disempowerment by strengthening a culture of Stewardship and justice for all

Small Group Discussion and Reflection

1. Review the definition of dominance and share one example of how "systems of privilege and preference reinforced by power" are functioning within personal interactions, professional relationships, or organizational practices in your school or organization.

    ⇨ Personal

    ⇨ Professional

    ⇨ Organizational

Section 2: Exploring the Streams of Engagement

2. Describe how at least one of the dynamics of dominance is at work within personal, professional, or organizational life in your school system, institution, or community.

Your Stories	Personal	Professional	Organizational
Luxury of Ignorance			
Assumption of Rightness			
Legacy of Privilege			

3. How might we work with these issues of privilege and power in ways that will create a more inclusive and welcoming learning/working environment and better outcomes for our students, colleagues, employees, and community?

4. Choose one of the issues of dominance and privilege negatively impacting the school culture.
- How would you approach dealing with it?

- Where would the resistance likely come from?

- What sources of support could you mobilize?

Personal Reflection

Know Self
- What emotions surfaced for you in this conversation?

- How did your own lived experiences influence your response?

- In what ways did you feel affirmed, challenged, or unsettled by what others shared?

Know Students
- What new insights did you gain about the lived realities of students who experience disempowerment in your school?

- How do these power dynamics affect students' academic, social, and emotional outcomes?

Know Practice
- How willing are your colleagues to engage honestly in this type of reflection?

- What structures or supports would help your team take this work deeper?

- How will you personally apply these insights to your classroom or leadership role?

Justice in the Words of Elders

"What love looks like in public."

– Cornel West

Description

As you may have discovered in your *Dominance to Justice Word Association* engagement, there are varying perspectives, political views, historical lenses, and personal experiences that color our understanding of the concept of justice. This is a good thing. A community of professional educators who mostly have the same view of what justice should look like in our schools is less prepared to deal with injustice than a community willing to acknowledge and understand multiple perspectives. The art of crafting a culture of Stewardship is not about indoctrinating others into a common doctrine of justice but rather about learning how to design and hold tight to a dynamic school vision and purpose—one that seeks balanced approaches for all children, holds students and adults accountable, and maintains a moral and ethical compass, all while allowing for a wide spectrum of views and beliefs.

In this engagement strategy, we bring in the voices of American elders who have been and still are fighting for justice in school spaces, in prison spaces, in nature spaces, and in the political arena. Listening to our elders reminds us we are not alone—that whatever struggles we are in today, someone has been there before us and learned something of value. Listening to our elders also offers us a perspective on the breadth and longevity of the struggle for equity and justice. As with any engagement in this book, the outcomes are always better served when you bring in additional voices from your community to help localize and broaden all that we are addressing when we talk about justice.

Learning Intentions

- Center the voices of American elders in our understanding of justice
- Reflect on diverse perspectives and historical experiences related to equity
- Identify personal connections to justice that shape your role as an educator
- Apply these reflections to support students and families in your school community

Personal Reflection

Read and reflect on the following quotes. Choose one of the quotes and reflect on these prompts. Be prepared to share out on one question.

- Why did you choose this quote?
- How is it relevant in your life and in your work?
- What is the relevance for students and families in our school?

What Is Justice?

"Charity is no substitute for justice. . . . We must never ignore the injustices that make charity necessary, or the inequalities that make it possible."
— Michael Eric Dyson

"It is never really won. You earn it and win it in every generation."
— Coretta Scott King

"The way we treat the earth is inseparable from the way our society treats women."
— Tracy Rector

"We're entitled to be loved, and seek happiness, and share that with the people that we care about."
— Miss Major Griffin-Gracy

Section 2: Exploring the Streams of Engagement

"The good of the many over the greed of a few."
— Gary Howard

"The opposite of poverty is justice."
— Bryan Stevenson

"We are not just fighting for a fair wage, we are fighting for dignity and respect in the workplace."
— Dolores Huerta

"Change doesn't come simply because we wish it."
— Sonia Nieto

Small Group Discussion

- Choose one quote you reflected on and share it out.
    - Why did you choose this quote?
    - How is it relevant in your life and in your work?
    - What is the relevance for students and families in our school?
- What themes emerged?
- How has your understanding of justice changed or been expanded?

Definition of Social Justice

Social justice is . . .
- Systems of equity and fairness
- Reinforced by respect and shared power
- Favoring the inclusion and well-being of all people

Compare and contrast the definitions of social dominance and social justice.
- What comes to mind?

- What would you add to this definition based on the voices of the elders and your own experiences?

Personal Reflection

Know Self
- What emotions or insights did the quotes evoke for you?

- How do your personal values align, or not, with the perspectives shared, and what did you learn from the discussion?

Know Students

- How can you bring intergenerational voices into your classroom to help students connect to justice?

- What messages about justice are your students receiving from your curriculum, your instruction, or your school culture?

Know Practice

- How do these reflections on justice shape your role as a steward in your school?

- What actions might you take to ensure that justice is not just spoken but felt by those you serve?

In My One Beat – Struggle

Description

This is an opportunity to take the In My One Beat poetry exercise we shared in Stream 2 and deepen the learning about our colleagues, our students, and ourselves (Colwell & Howard, 2018). The structure is the same as in Stream 2—every line begins with the words; In my One Beat. Now the challenge is to imagine your struggle, the hard parts of your life, the difficulties you have endured and overcome as part of your strength, and how your contribution as a creative being, as a Steward, is fortified by the life you have experienced. This is an opportunity to take the learning from our conversations about the dynamics of dominance and our experiences with power and privilege, and take those from the level of the head to the level of the heart. This is a courageous opportunity to bring to life the key components of stewardship: care and knowledge. With good facilitation and good support, this experience will deepen your professional capacities on all three sides of the Achievement Triangle.

Note: This kind of courageous, creative conversation needs intentional and sometimes professional support around it when engaging adults or students. There needs to be a unanimous consensus that the Community Agreements you generated in Stream 1 are honored and that there is a level of trust in the learning space that allows for vulnerability and courageous storytelling. There may be power dynamics at play that don't allow people to feel comfortable engaging at this level. Permission always needs to be given to those people who are not comfortable or feel threatened to express that truth, or simply opt out.

Learning Intentions

- Express experiences of struggle through storytelling and poetry
- Deepen understanding of the personal impact of power, privilege, and resistance
- Honor vulnerability as a courageous act of Stewardship and healing
- Use creative expression as a form of cultural identity and community connection

Section 2: Exploring the Streams of Engagement

Example poem from a student in Reading, Pennsylvania

> In my one beat I am targeted, afraid to look a cop in the eye
> In my one beat people cross the street when I come into view
> In my one beat I want to be successful but I have many obstacles
> In my one beat I watch my mom struggle to make the rent and take care of all of us and eventually reaching her goal
> In my one beat it inspires me to reach with her

In My One Beat, my struggle is like . . .

Personal Reflection

Know Self

- What have you learned about your personal courage throughout the more challenging aspects of this work?

- What did it feel like to name or share your struggle?

Know Team

- What did you learn by hearing the stories and poems of others?

- How might these glimpses into others' truths affect your professional relationships and team culture?

Know Practice

- What is the value of making our individual and collective struggles more visible in education spaces?

- How can this practice of storytelling help you grow a more equitable, caring, and just learning environment?

In My One Beat - Struggle developed in collaboration with W.A. Colwell

What are you thinking? What do you want to remember?

Stream 4: Intergenerational Partnership & Practice

"When someone with the authority of a teacher describes the world and you are not in it, there is a moment of psychic disequilibrium, as if you looked into a mirror and saw nothing."

– Adrienne Rich

In Stream 4, we bring the work we've done together in the other streams and apply it directly to our professional practices. The *Achievement Triangle* and the *Definition of Cultural Competence* illustrate that an Empowered Steward has the courage and grace to critically examine one's own beliefs and assumptions while also demonstrating the will and ability to create relationships across the diversity of lenses found in our school ecosystems. The transformation toward equitable classroom practices is about more than learning specific instructional strategies that are found to be effective with diverse groups of students; it also requires that we know ourselves and our students at a deeper level. The climate of trust you established in Stream 1, the depth of conversations about your personal culture in Stream 2, and your honest consideration of privilege and social dominance issues in Stream 3 all impact the effectiveness of your Stream 4 efforts.

The work in Stream 4 must be approached with deep acknowledgment and respect for the good things you and your team are already doing. As we discussed in the introduction to this guidebook, there is a profound need for healing and affirmation among school employees, who have too often felt under siege by the demands and punitive consequences of top-down school reform policies. In our Stream 4 work, we honor our own and your teammates' good intentions and professionalism, while at the same time challenging ourselves to critically examine how some of our own behaviors, beliefs, and practices may be getting in the way of the change we envision.

Stream 4 provides a practical, integrative framework for all of the work you are presently doing on school improvement and strengthening instruction. The *Seven Commitments of Stewardship* are the core conceptual and pedagogical content for this phase of the work. For team members who may feel overwhelmed or unfocused because of the multiple professional development and instructional initiatives that have accompanied school reform mandates, these Seven Commitments can help unify their efforts. The commitments are an effective tool for assessing our practice, and they are a powerful set of guidelines for directing and inspiring professional growth. Stream 4's work with the commitments will lay a solid foundation for collegial collaboration, wherein faculty and staff can willingly share their strengths and skills with each other, as well as courageously acknowledge their struggles and their fears. These activities can recharge our pedagogical batteries, make sense of our work, provide direction for our professional improvement, and validate the many good things we are already doing. Our hope and intention in Stream 4 is to engender for ourselves that state of self-generated neuroplasticity that leads us to say, "I know I am a good professional, and for that reason I want to push back against any of the barriers I may be putting in the way of other's success, especially for those who are most different from me."

The engagement activities in Stream 4 will give your team members opportunities to work individually and collectively on research-based strategies shown to be effective with diverse groups of students. Team members will be able to access their own areas of strength and growth and identify an area of focus aligned with their *School Outcomes Assessment* focus areas. This stream is deeply rooted in a robust research base, emphasizing that the more we put these practices into action, the more we learn and evolve. Over time, our language and approaches have progressed since the early beginnings of this work—rooted in the multicultural education movement—to a more explicit understanding of culturally responsive pedagogy, driven by Gloria Ladson-Billings, Geneva Gay, and many other scholars and practitioners.

- When students see their own cultures reflected in the curriculum and instructional materials, they are more likely to feel connected to the content and motivated to participate actively in their learning (Gay, 2018; Ladson-Billings, 1994).

- When students' cultures and languages are affirmed in the classroom, they are more likely to engage deeply and meaningfully with their learning. This affirmation leads to a sense of belonging and empowerment, allowing students to see their cultural identities as assets rather than obstacles (González et al., 2005; Paris & Alim, 2017).

- By promoting cultural competence, empathy, and respect for diversity, educators can equip students with the knowledge, skills, and attitudes needed to succeed in a globalized world (Banks, 2016; Sleeter, 2003).

Community Recitation Poem (English/Spanish)

We can build an environment together every day
Where each student, staff, and family member would say
They understand me. I am welcomed. I am reflected.
They celebrate me. I am valued. I am respected.
Learning is about self and community well-being.
Every day, my school is uplifting & freeing.

Podemos construir juntos un ambiente todos los días
donde cada alumno, empleado y familiar diría,
Me entienden. Soy bienvenido. Soy reflejado.
Me celebran. Soy valorado. Soy respetado.
Aprender es sobre el bienestar propio y comunitario.
La escuela me edifica y me libera a diario.

Overview of Engagement Strategies

Stream 4 engagement strategies build shared leadership through culturally responsive and intergenerational practice. Centering the Seven Commitments of Stewardship, these strategies help teams co-create inclusive learning environments that honor student voice, educator agency, and community wisdom. They promote collaborative inquiry as a cycle of action and reflection rooted in mutual accountability and learning across generations. See the table below for engagement strategies that advance equity through collective practice.

Layers of Engagement

Stream 4 promotes culturally responsive practice and shared leadership through intentional intergenerational collaboration. At the personal level, educators engage in self-assessment and action research to deepen their understanding of the Seven Stewardship Commitments. At the professional level, teams function as learning communities where colleagues and students co-design and test equity-centered strategies. At the organizational level, these partnerships become embedded into the fabric of school culture, sustaining inclusive, student-driven improvement. This stream models how lasting transformation depends on collective agency and accountability across generations, ultimately pushing back on structural norms that isolate decision-making from those most impacted.

Engagements that Support Collaborative Inquiry

The YES Collaborative Inquiry Process fuels this stream by embedding student voice and educator collaboration into cycles of co-designed action research. Inquiry becomes a shared practice across generations—students, educators, and families analyzing impact, iterating on strategies, and sustaining equitable change. The engagements in Stream 4 highlight the importance of placing students' voices at the core of educational development, ensuring that teaching practices are not only effective but also equitable and responsive to diverse cultural contexts. All engagements in this stream support the Yes Collaborative Inquiry process and the action research projects are closely tied to the 2nd phase for empathizing and deepening awareness the 5th and 6th phases involving prototyping and co-creation and investigating and evaluating. Once engaged in the action research projects, they support all six phases and provide insights that revise existing or begin new inquiry. In addition to these connections, Table 5: Applying the Engagements of Stream 4 illustrates how collaborative inquiry occurs across personal, professional, and organizational dimensions.

Section 2: Exploring the Streams of Engagement

Key Engagements in Stream 4:

- **The Seven Stewardship Commitments:** This is the central conceptual framework for Empowered Stewardship professional practice. Through your inquiry process, you will be identifying groups of students, families, and colleagues to focus your inquiry on. You will identify a puzzle of practice to solve through inquiry, and you will be maintaining professional learning in at least one of the 7 commitments. All of the engagement strategies in Stream 4 should be explored regularly and with particular attention to your inquiry focus group/s.
- **Learning From and With Colleagues:** is a great place to start. (All Inquiry)

Table 5: Applying the Engagements of Stream 4

Strategy	Collaborative Inquiry	Personal (Individual)	Professional (Team)	Organizational (System)
Seven Commitments Study Groups	•			•
Seven Commitments Assessment	•	•	•	•
Learning From and With Colleagues		•	•	•
Glow and Grow: Student Reflection on Teacher Practice	•	•	•	•
Seven Commitments Action Research Project		•	•	•
Seven Commitments Student-Centered Project		•	•	•

Introducing the Seven Commitments of Stewardship Practice

The *Seven Commitments of Stewardship* (shown in Figure 17), which are centered in all of the Stream 4 engagement strategies, bring us to another aspect of the *Achievement Triangle*, this time focusing on the base of the triangle: *Knowing My Practice*. This asks us to continually deepen our knowledge of professional practices, ensuring we are providing research-based strategies that maximize equitable and inclusive support. These commitments, impacting all of the rooms in the House of Learning (see Figure 18), elevate the work you have been doing throughout the Stewardship process.

Figure 17: Seven Commitments of Stewardship

	1. Our cultural identities are affirmed and valued
	2. Our relationships are rooted in earned respect and cultural humility
	3. Our learning environments are inviting, culturally relevant, and vibrant
	4. Our expectations and actions amplify adult and student brilliance
	5. Our interactions celebrate and adapt to diverse ways of knowing, learning, and being
	6. Our educational experiences reinforce creative and critical thinking
	7. Our interactions honor individual aspirations and collective responsibilities

Source: Inspired by and adapted from Shade et al., 1997. Used with permission.

Invitation Into the House of Learning

The seven commitments are organized into three aspects. Commitments 1, 2, and 3 are considered the **Front Porch**. Imagine a house in the South, where families sit on chairs or on a bench on the front porch, wave to people passing by, invite guests up for tea or a glass of water, and greet family when they come to visit. Imagine the stoop at the front of a row house in Philadelphia in the summertime, where life spills out into the street and neighbors connect. The Front Porch commitments are the invitation into the House of Learning. They represent how the bus driver welcomes children onto the bus, how family members and visitors are welcomed at the front office of the school, and how hallways represent the cultural realities of students and staff, the understanding that as students, colleagues, and families, we are seen, understood, and valued in the school environment.

Commitments 4 and 5 are considered the **Kitchen**. Imagine cupboards full of ingredients, a fridge stocked with fresh produce, drawers filled with utensils, and a shelf lined with cookbooks. A kitchen is a place that holds the possibility of wonderful meals. This is where we cook up the belief that every child, every scholar, and every professional is brilliant and has infinite potential. And beyond belief, it is the ability to cook with, dance with, or sing harmony with a child or a colleague's brilliance. It's where we make it all happen together.

Commitments 6 and 7 are considered the **Table**. Picture yourself sitting down at a long table filled with beautiful dishes, surrounded by family and friends. Imagine the conversation. As a metaphor, this is where we get down to the business of what we learn, how we learn, and what it means to be an educated person in society. The table holds the bounty of the land. It is the table of the possibility of democracy. It is the table of the possibility of democracy. These two commitments allow educators to reflect on and amplify our practice with regard to preparing students to live in the world, equipping them to work creatively, think critically, and be resilient, and to give back while caring for themselves, their families, their communities, and the land.

Figure 18: The House of Learning

Seven Commitments From Multiple Lenses: What Students, Teachers, Families, and Leaders Say

1. **Our Cultural Identities Are Affirmed and Valued**
    - **Teachers say:** I affirm and value each student's and family's identities. I seek deeper understanding.
    - **Students say:** I get it that my teacher gets me and my family.
    - **Families say:** My child's identity and our family's culture are affirmed and valued in this school.
    - **Leaders say:** I recognize and affirm the value of each talent and perspective that the adults, students, and families in our building bring. I intentionally create space for these talents and cultures to resonate throughout our school.

2. **Our Relationships Are Rooted in Earned Respect and Cultural Humility**
    - **Teachers say:** I earn students' and families' respect. I am curious and know that I have a lot to learn from my students and their families.
    - **Students say:** I get it that my teacher sees me and respects me and my family.
    - **Families say:** I feel welcomed, respected, and heard in my child's school.
    - **Leaders say:** I earn my staff's and families' respect. I am curious and know that I have a lot to learn from my teachers, staff, students, and their families. My greatest expression of respect is honoring their voices as essential partners in learning.

3. **Our Learning Environments Are Inviting, Culturally Relevant, and Vibrant**
    - **Teachers say:** My classroom is vibrant and colorful. It represents the lives and cultural realities of my students and their families. It feels like a home for all.
    - **Students say:** School is exciting and feels like a home for me and my family.
    - **Families say:** When I walk into my child's school, I see our culture, language, and values reflected in the environment.
    - **Leaders say:** Our school is vibrant and inclusive. It represents the lives and cultural realities of our staff, students, and families, creating an environment where everyone can show up transparent and authentic.

4. **Our Expectations and Actions Amplify Adult, Student, and Family Brilliance**
   - **Teachers say:** I honestly and authentically believe in the capacity and brilliance of all my students and their families. I am a loving and "warm demander."
   - **Students say:** My teacher believes I am brilliant.
   - **Families say:** My child's teacher sees their brilliance and values our family's funds of knowledge.
   - **Leaders say:** I genuinely and authentically believe in the capacity and brilliance of all my staff, students, and families. I look for and assess the values of our school in each teacher, staff member, and family partnership that we build. I am supportive and a "warm demander."

5. **Our Interactions Celebrate and Adapt to Diverse Ways of Knowing, Learning, and Being**
   - **Teachers say:** I am always growing my care and knowledge, and adjusting my practice in order to align with students' and families' brilliance.
   - **Students say:** My teacher can sing harmony with my unique way of being brilliant.
   - **Families say:** My child's teacher respects the way we learn, communicate, and navigate the world.
   - **Leaders say:** I am always growing my care and knowledge, and adjusting my leadership practices to align with my staff's and families' brilliance. I am a student of my community.

6. **Our Educational Experiences Reinforce Creative and Critical Thinking**
   - **Teachers say:** I am ever cognizant that in every lesson there is an opportunity for real-world relevance, for students' outside-the-box thinking and creative expression, and for deep critical thinking about learning, power, and equity.
   - **Students say:** I am learning how to think for myself, to be creative, and to question things.
   - **Families say:** My child is encouraged to think critically, ask questions, and express themselves creatively.
   - **Leaders say:** I am ever cognizant that in every interaction there is an opportunity for real-world relevance, for my staff's and families' outside-the-box thinking and creative expression, and for deep reflection on learning, power, and equity.

Section 2: Exploring the Streams of Engagement

7. **Our Interactions Honor Individual Aspirations and Collective Responsibilities**
    - **Teachers say:** My practice nurtures both individual and collective ways of learning, ensuring students grow into their personal aspirations while embracing their responsibility to uplift and be stewards in their communities.
    - **Students say:** I am supported in reaching my goals while also learning how to give back to my family, my community, humanity, and the land. My learning is interconnected with the growth and success of others.
    - **Families say:** Our family's hopes, dreams, and cultural values are woven into our child's education, fostering both personal success and collective well-being.
    - **Leaders say:** My leadership fosters a culture where both individual aspirations and collective responsibility thrive. I prepare my staff to lead, learn, and contribute in ways that strengthen our professional community and our partnerships with families.

Seven Commitments Application: Growing Classroom Practice, Classroom Culture

Think of The Seven Commitments as the on-ramp to growing practice as individual professionals and as communities of professional learners. As we do the work of growing together within our professional learning groups and across roles and departments, we take part in the work of growing collective efficacy and a culture of Stewardship. The examples of surface, shallow, and deep applications below in Figure 19 are real examples from schools we have worked with over the past decade. Think of surface applications as entry-level classroom practice; applications that celebrate culture, identity, and brilliance, but may require lower levels of personal or professional risk. Think of Shallow applications as taking a step toward greater understanding and challenging biases and norms that can get in the way of serving kids and colleagues. Think of deep applications as individual and systemic moves that allow for deeper understanding, reconciliation, and transformative practice. The examples should support you in a discussion that begins with celebrating the good work you are already doing and moving toward deeper application that serves to meet the needs of more students, across more of their differences, more of the time, without requiring that they give up any aspects of their cultural identities.

Section 2: Exploring the Streams of Engagement

Figure 19: Seven Commitments Sample Applications

Commitment	Surface	Shallow	Deep
1. Our cultural identities are affirmed and valued	Administrators make a decision to install flags in the lunchroom that represent the nationalities of students in the school.	Efforts are made to celebrate and acknowledge the diversity of nationalities/ethnicities in the school community throughout the school year. Efforts are made to grow awareness of community events and celebrations. Words from multiple languages are regularly shared.	Palestinian high school students paint a rock on campus in the colors of the Palestinian flag. Students, teachers, and administrators enter into a restorative dialogue about how to create safe and productive learning spaces for Palestinian students from immigrant families and students from Jewish families in the community.
2. Our relationships are rooted in earned respect and cultural humility	Teachers engage students in co-constructing Community Agreements for classrooms at the beginning of the school year.	Teachers and students co-construct protocols for holding themselves and each other accountable to the Community Agreements.	The entire school community engages in a year-long process to replace existing rules and norms with Community Agreements and accountability structures with input from leaders, teachers, students, staff, and families. Measures are taken to review and revise annually, and bring in new hires and new students into the process.

Commitment	Surface	Shallow	Deep
3. Our learning environments are inviting, culturally relevant, and vibrant	Colorful classrooms, student art in hallways, and posters of diverse authors, artists, and historical figures hang on the walls.	A school, in an effort to transcend the traditional orientation around Dr. Martin Luther King and Rosa Parks during Black History Month, brings in more current voices, from Kendrick Lamar, Nikole Hannah-Jones, Amanda Gorman, and others.	The entire school community engages in a year-long process to replace existing rules and norms with Community Agreements and accountability structures with input from leaders, teachers, students, staff, and families. Measures are taken to review and revise annually, and bring in new hires and new students into the process.
4. Our expectations and actions amplify adult and student brilliance	The principal has a poster on the wall stating that "we believe every child is brilliant."	Individual acts of brilliance are celebrated by posting essays, hanging up good works, gold stars for students, awards to teachers, public acknowledgment of principals' achievements, articles, and social media posts.	Classroom student surveys are gathered across a district to assess how many students authentically believe their teachers know they are smart. Survey data include student perspectives on teacher actions and behaviors, indicating belief or lack of belief in their intelligence. Students are invited into a puzzle of practice inquiry on educator efficacy.

Section 2: Exploring the Streams of Engagement

Commitment	Surface	Shallow	Deep
5. Our interactions celebrate and adapt to diverse ways of knowing, learning, and being	Educators are using varying readability materials, presenting ideas via auditory and visual means, reading buddies, student-led re-teaching, and small group learning.	The school and district have invested in a robust ecosystem of professional specialists: school counselors, psychologists, occupational therapists, media specialists, speech language pathologists, translators, and others.	All teachers in a building spend the first 2 weeks of school focusing on getting to know students, sharing In My One Beat poems, bringing in artifacts from home and culture, learning greetings in multiple languages, sharing music, asking students how they love to learn, and inviting families. Throughout the school year, teachers utilize PLC time to identify students who are struggling to reach and teach, and share strategies, best practices, and breakthroughs.

Commitment	Surface	Shallow	Deep
6. Our educational experiences reinforce creative and critical thinking	Multiple perspectives and diverse viewpoints are discussed and debated within Civics courses, global issues courses, history courses, and arts-integrated curriculum.	The racial, ethnic, cultural, linguistic, and gender diversity of your student population is reflected, acknowledged, and honored in general ethnic studies courses, Mexican American Studies, Black History, Indigenous History, and Women's History courses.	Students in a high school are invited to an end-of-school-year review of the social studies curriculum. They are asked the following questions: Whose stories did you learn about in class? Which stories were most prominent? Which stories were missing? What ideas stood out for you? Who benefits from those ideas? Who does not? How? What literature should be included next year? New curriculum adoption is informed by student perspectives.
7. Our interactions honor individual aspirations and collective responsibilities	Individualized learning plans provide opportunities for group projects and group learning.	Acts of Stewardship and care for others are recognized and celebrated. Stewardship is established as a frame for school ethics and culture, and as a frame for how the school community defines educational excellence. Mission and vision statements are revised to include Stewardship.	Pre-K through 12th grade First Nations and Indigenous language first approaches in New Zealand, British Columbia, and in Navajo schools in Arizona and New Mexico all include some version of the following definition of educational excellence: "An educated or learned person is someone who has gained the knowledge, skills and moral capacities to give back to the communities that raised them."

Seven Commitments Study Groups

Description

As you work through the engagement strategies in Stream 4, engagements address the student focus group(s) you and your colleagues have selected (refer to the *School Outcomes Assessment*). This activity will enable you to identify strengths and areas of growth related to the *Seven Commitments of Stewardship* with the focus group of students in mind.

This activity allows your team to gather reciprocal feedback from key groups of partners (youth, colleagues, parents).

Focus Group: _____

With these students in mind, this jigsaw activity gives your team an opportunity to work with the Stewardship Commitments. Individually and collectively, team members will have opportunities to create connections between current practices in the school ecosystem that exemplify each of the Stewardship Commitments. Teams will collect examples of the commitments in action and suggestions for how to expand your impact.

What you identify as your colleagues' areas of strength, as well as the information regarding individual and group members' areas of growth, can be used by teams to make future decisions regarding your Stewardship action steps.

Learning Intentions

- Deepen understanding of the *Seven Commitments of Stewardship* practice
- Determine strengths and opportunities for growth regarding the *Seven Commitments of Stewardship*
- Identify specific practices and adult actions that support or hinder each of the Seven Commitments

Home Group

When working through this engagement in large groups, we recommend you form groups of seven people with each one dedicating their attention to a different Stewardship Commitment. However, the point of the activity is to reflect on the commitments in relation to your student focus group. Divide up the commitments in a way that ensures members have the time they need to fully engage in the activity, even if this means coming back to certain commitments during another session.

"Expert" Group

Find others in the room or group who have selected the same commitment.
Collectively, answer the following:

- Restate the commitment by underlining key words and identifying a synonym for each.
- What does this look like, feel like, or sound like in interactions?
- What is an example of this commitment at a surface level, a shallow level, or a deep level of engagement? (Reference the Seven Commitments Sample Applications in Figure 19.)
- What is one idea to move this commitment to a deeper level?

Section 2: Exploring the Streams of Engagement

Seven Commitments Study Groups Template

Paraphrase Your Commitment 1 2 3 4 5 6 7 (circle)		
Identify examples of how to apply this Commitment at each level.		
Surface	Shallow	Deep
What is one idea to move this commitment to a deeper level?		

Visit the Stream 4 Resources on our website for an example of Seven Commitments Study Groups

Home Group

Return to your original group. Each person will have 2 to 3 minutes to share responses regarding the paraphrased commitment, an example of it in action, and a way its application could be deepened. Use the chart above to summarize your learning as a group.

This activity can be adapted to PLCs, equity teams, or other small groups.

Personal Reflection

Know Self
- Which of the Seven Commitments do you most naturally embody in your day-to-day actions?

- Which commitment feels most challenging or uncomfortable for you to apply, and why?

Know Students
- Which commitments do your students experience most clearly in your learning environment?

- How do students in your identified focus group define or demonstrate hope, care, or power?

Know Practice
- What specific systems or routines in your classroom or school reflect the Seven Commitments in action?

- Where in your practice could you deepen from surface or shallow applications of a commitment to something more transformative?

Seven Commitments Assessment

Description

In this engagement, members of the team are invited to assess their own professional practices related to the *Seven Commitments of Stewardship*. Use the self-assessment below to reflect on the Seven Commitments and your own professional practices. Circle the commitment you will name as your Strength Commitment and which is your Growth Commitment.

For each of the *Seven Commitments of Stewardship*, give yourself a 1–10 rating indicating how well you feel you are doing in implementing the intent of that Commitment.

1. My students' cultural identities are affirmed and valued.

    1   2   3   4   5   6   7   8   9   10

2. My relationships with students are rooted in earned respect and cultural humility.

    1   2   3   4   5   6   7   8   9   10

3. Our learning environments are inviting, culturally relevant, and vibrant.

    1   2   3   4   5   6   7   8   9   10

4. Our expectations and actions amplify adult and student brilliance.

    1   2   3   4   5   6   7   8   9   10

5. Our interactions celebrate and adapt to diverse ways of knowing, learning, and being.

   1   2   3   4   5   6   7   8   9   10

6. Our educational experiences reinforce creative and critical thinking.

   1   2   3   4   5   6   7   8   9   10

7. Our interactions honor individual aspirations and collective responsibilities.

   1   2   3   4   5   6   7   8   9   10

Based on the self-assessment:

Strength: In which Commitment are you the strongest?

Growth: For which Commitment would you most like to grow your effectiveness?

Personal Reflection

Know Self
- How does your *strength* commitment show up in your practice?

- What's getting in the way of your *growth* commitment?

Know Students
- How might your knowledge of your students, individually and collectively, impact how you proceed in strengthening the *growth* commitment you chose?

Know Practice
- What do you need to support your growth in this commitment?

Learning From and With Colleagues

"Alone, we can do so little; together, we can do so much."

– Helen Keller

Description

This engagement continues our work connected to the base of the *Achievement Triangle* – Knowing My Practice. The goal here is to deepen our working knowledge of the *Seven Commitments of Stewardship*. While we are primarily focusing on the base of the *Achievement Triangle*, it is also important to keep in mind the other two sides of that triangle: Knowing Myself and Knowing My Students. Those two dimensions of quality classroom practice are essential and foundational elements for the Stream 4 work.

In all Stream 4 engagement activities, you are encouraged to reflect on the focus groups identified in the School Outcomes Assessment in Stream 1. This engagement fosters conversations deeply rooted in the daily work your teams are doing in schools to support equity and inclusion. Creating a supportive environment for growth, team members will get opportunities to showcase their efforts in promoting equity and inclusion within their buildings. In alignment with the *Seven Commitments of Stewardship* and the levels of culturally responsive practices, teams will work together to identify examples of surface, shallow, and deep practices that could support the members of your school ecosystem. In the Stewardship way, team members will develop a deeper understanding of the Seven Commitments, identify multiple examples of each commitment in action, and discuss the current systems that are in place to grow this work.

Learning Intentions

- Deepen your work with the *Seven Commitments of Stewardship*
- Create a climate focused on mutual growth and support
- Discuss real-life struggles connected to equity and inclusion
- Collectively generate actionable next steps for addressing these struggles

Gallery Walk
Prior to this engagement, determine a process for gathering notes from each of the small group discussions.

Round One: Stewardship Strength Commitment # _____
Gather with others who are strong in this commitment. Brainstorm what you are already doing in your practice that is reinforcing this Commitment. Record 3-5 of these teacher practices.

To go deeper, review the list you have generated to discuss whether examples are surface, shallow, or deep.

Round Two: Stewardship Growth Commitment # _____
Gather with others who want to grow in this commitment. Brainstorm the things you are doing in your practice that are reinforcing this Commitment. Record 3-5 of these teacher practices.

To go deeper, review the list you have generated to discuss whether examples are surface, shallow, or deep.

Personal Reflection
Thinking about your own growth commitment and the focus groups with whom you want to expand your impact, what are the possible next steps you can take to grow your knowledge and skills related to this commitment?

- Possible Action Step Today:

- Possible Action Step This Month:

- Possible Action Step This Year:

Glow and Grow: Student Reflections on Teacher Practice

Description

The *Glow and Grow* engagement is an opportunity to include students in a conversation about how we can all celebrate strong Stewardship practice, and how we can invite student perspective into how we think about expanding and deepening our practice as educators. Using the *Seven Commitments of Stewardship* as a rubric, we invite students into a conversation about what it looks like and feels like to be authentically welcomed into the House of Learning (the Front Porch: Commitments 1-3), what it looks and feels like to know without question that a teacher believes in and can dance with their particular brilliance (the Kitchen: Commitments 4 and 5), and what it looks and feels like when respect is earned, classroom culture is established, and instruction is delivered in ways that align with a student's personal and cultural ways of being (the Table: Commitments 6 and 7). This engagement is also an opportunity to get real data from students about how we, as educators, can improve our practice.

The challenge here is that the engagement requires adults to receive evaluation feedback from the very people we are used to evaluating. The fear is often that students might use the opportunity merely to complain about adults, which can happen, of course, and when it does, remind yourself that adults complain about students, too! This engagement, however, is not designed to register complaints, but rather it is an opportunity for adults and students to engage in honest, courageous conversation about what we can celebrate and how we can grow our practice.

This requires some foundation building of trust, which is the work of Stream 2. Having some level of intergenerational care and knowledge, respect for one another's humanity, and some level of trust based on the understanding of each other's stories, all of this Stream 2 work, is critical in order for the conversation to be productive. It also has strong Stream 3 implications as it is an exercise in sharing power. When facilitated with care and intention, it represents a challenge to traditional power structures in school and absolutely requires educators to not only listen to students but make changes based on what we learn. Otherwise, if it's just listening and not doing, we run the risk of disempowering our students.

Notes From the Field:

- We've implemented this engagement with 4th- through 12th-grade students, principals, counselors, and district administrators.

- In our experience, students have much more positive things to say about teacher practice than negative things to say.

- In general, educators who are willing to receive student feedback have stronger relationships with students and, therefore, a greater impact on student success (Hattie, 2012; Roorda et al., 2011; Wiggins, 2012).

Learning Intentions

- Invite student perspectives into the work of growing educator excellence
- Increase capacity for knowledge of and care for students' educational experience
- Empower students as co-creators of successful learning environments
- Increase culturally responsive and Stewardship practice

Glow and Grow Student Comments Template for The Front Porch (Commitments 1-3)

The Front Porch
- Commitment 1: I get it that teachers get me. - Commitment 2: I get it that teachers see me and earn my respect. - Commitment 3: School feels exciting, welcoming, and real.

Student Report From Small Group Dialogue on the "Front Porch"	
What Glows?	**How Can We Grow?**
What actions, practices, ways of being, or classroom design make you excited and welcome when you enter the House of Learning?	What actions, practices, and behaviors make the Front Porch uninviting, make it difficult to enter the House of Learning?

Section 2: Exploring the Streams of Engagement

Example Glow and Grow Student Comments for The Front Porch (Commitments 1-3)

The Front Porch

- Commitment 1: I get it that teachers get me.
- Commitment 2: I get it that teachers see me and earn my respect.
- Commitment 3: School feels exciting, welcoming, and real.

Student Report Examples for Commitments 1–3 from Students in the Auburn School District in Washington State

What Glows?	How Can We Grow?
• "Taking the time to get to know students. I know it's hard, but you can do it." • "Knowing my struggle" • "Color, light, music, my language" • "I know it when a teacher really wants to have a relationship with me." • "Meeting us at the door every day" • "I miss Venezuela. Pictures are everything." • "I think curiosity is the thing. You don't need to know everything about me, just be curious—then I know you can respect me." • "I have this teacher who knows that I'm taking care of my little brother. Sometimes he's more important than getting my homework in on time. She knows that." • "Teachers here know that some of us are the only responsible person in our lives. It doesn't look like responsibility to some people, but they know.	• "Making assumptions about our lives or our background" • "Flags and food are not enough to make me feel at home at school. It takes more for me to know this is a home." • "It's not always what you say, it's the tone that tells me I'm not welcome." • "I know teachers have to be professional, but sometimes it's like too professional, you know?" • "Sometimes I feel like I'm in trouble before I say anything." • "My headphones are respected by some teachers and not others. I need them. I need isolation to learn." • "I feel for teachers. It seems like a hard job, but sometimes I think they get burned out, and we are just like faces."

Glow and Grow Student Comments Template for The Kitchen (Commitments 4-5)

The Kitchen
- Commitment 4: Teachers believe in my unique brilliance. - Commitment 5: Teachers can harmonize with my brilliance.

Student Report From Small Group Dialogue on the "Kitchen"

What Glows?	How Can We Grow?
What does it look and feel like when teachers/educators believe in your brilliance and can dance with, or harmonize with, your intelligence?	What does it look and feel like when teachers don't see you as brilliant, or can't dance with your particular way of being smart?

Section 2: Exploring the Streams of Engagement

Example Glow and Grow Student Comments for The Kitchen (Commitments 4-5)

The Kitchen
• Commitment 4: Teachers believe in my unique brilliance. • Commitment 5: Teachers can harmonize with my brilliance.

Student Report Examples for Commitments 4 and 5 From Upper Darby High School, Pennsylvania, and DuPage 88 SD, Illinois:

What Glows?	How Can We Grow?
• "Teachers provide the ingredients, but it's the students who do the cooking." • "Teachers can just ask us what we need to learn or how we learn. Most of us know." • "I grew up in West Englewood, where violence was a thing. Out here (Chicago suburbs), it's a different thing, like the violence of language and looks. Knowing these two worlds is my kind of wisdom." • "The belief part can't be just one teacher. It has to be part of the culture." • "Making subjects relevant and exciting unlocks our intelligence." • "When a teacher sings in harmony with your intelligence, it's hard to describe, but you know it. It's something you have to feel."	• "When one teacher finds the key to reach a kid's intelligence, it has to be shared with other teachers." • "You can't believe in a student's brilliance if you don't even know who they are." • "Teaching to standards, not to people" • "Teachers sometimes don't understand that school is a life and death situation for me." • "Getting things wrong should be a good thing, part of learning, not punished."

Glow and Grow Student Comments Template for The Table (Commitments 6-7)

The Table
• Commitment 6: I am learning how to think for myself, to be creative, and to question things. • Commitment 7: I am being prepared to reach my goals and to give back to my family, my community, humanity, and the land. I am responsible for my own learning and for others to learn.
Student Report From Small Group Dialogue on the "Table"

What Glows?	How Can We Grow?
What does it look and feel like when teachers inspire you to think creatively and critically? What does it mean to be an educated person?	What does it look and feel like when teachers do not inspire you to think creatively and critically? What does it mean to be an educated person?

Section 2: Exploring the Streams of Engagement

Example Glow and Grow Student Comments for The Table (Commitments 6-7)

The Table

- Commitment 6: I am learning how to think for myself, to be creative, and to question things.
- Commitment 7: I am being prepared to reach my goals and to give back to my family, my community, humanity, and the land. I am responsible for my own learning and for others to learn.

Student Report Examples for Commitments 6 and 7 From Auburn School District, Washington:

What Glows?	How Can We Grow?
• "History gets so much more interesting when you get to hear stories about people who don't normally show up in the stuff you read." • We are working in groups right now to come up with solutions to real-world problems. I learned that educating women is a top factor in raising communities out of poverty. It's like we can really do something about it now." • "If I succeed, it's not just for me. I want to be the first person to go to college. It's for my family. It's for my Muckleshoot Nation." • Being educated means I'm prepared to live in the world now, not the world of 30 years ago."	• "Get rid of rows. No more rows. And while we're at it, what's up with grades? Why do we have to be stratified before we even know who we are?" • "Why do I get in trouble for looking at my neighbor's work? Aren't we smarter together?" • "When teachers pretend that they are neutral politically, it feels dishonest." • "I liked how they shared the idea that the solutions to the problems we face are right here in the community where people are impacted. Mostly, I don't think we're taught that we have good ideas or solutions."

Small Group Discussion

- What is the readiness level in order to have these kinds of reflective conversations with students in your school/district?
- What existing structures, if any, does your school/district have in place to collect data regarding student perspectives on teacher practice?
- If so, what is the structure and what have you learned?
- How might this structure, with this Seven Commitments rubric, be applied?
- What seems challenging about this?

Personal Reflection

Know Self

- What did you feel as you heard students' glows and grows?
- Where have you seen evidence of your own growth? What specific incidents can you name?

Know Students

- What story or student interaction comes to mind that reflects progress in your practice?

Know Practice

- How might you respond to student feedback?
- What would it take to build a classroom culture where student voice shapes your teaching?

Visit the Stream 4 Resources on our website for examples of Glow and Grow Student Comments

Seven Commitments Action Research Project

Description

Stream 4 has given you and your team a variety of opportunities to engage in conversations about the *Seven Commitments of Stewardship* and how they show up in your professional practices and systems. Individuals have assessed their personal practices related to the *Seven Commitments*, as well as discussed what's currently happening in terms of both doorways and barriers in their classrooms and schools. Hopefully by this time, you have also listened to and recorded student voices and learned from their perspectives on your professional practices. In this engagement, you and each of your colleagues are invited to create a personal *Seven Commitments Action Research Project* related to one of the *Seven Commitments of Stewardship*. In this way, you will be able to deepen your practice related to the student groups you identified in the *School Outcomes Assessment*.

By this point in the Stewardship process, everyone on your team has selected a Strength Commitment, which represents one of their areas of professional strength, and a Growth Commitment, which is an area of practice they would like to improve. In this way, everyone in your team will be stretching their professional muscles, moving the body of their practice in new ways, and exercising that "self-generated neuroplasticity" discussed in the introduction to this guidebook.

This project is structured using collaborative inquiry, though in a compacted form. Together, you and your compatriots will notice and disrupt patterns that inhibit student belonging and success, deepen awareness through empathy-driven dialogue, reframe challenges using evidence, imagine bold possibilities, and prototype and co-create more equitable practices. Ultimately, you will evaluate and sustain your efforts by assessing impact and ensuring that students and families are co-authors of change.

This collaborative action research process can also be incorporated into your annual professional growth plans and can be revisited in subsequent years, with different professional practice outcome goals each time.

Learning Intentions

- Design and implement a *Seven Commitments Action Research Project* to improve your practice related to your Growth Commitment
- Strengthen your effectiveness with student groups that have been historically marginalized or underserved
- Foster a mutually supportive climate of shared growth among adults in your school
- Focus on collectively improving your effectiveness with those groups of students you have been "missing or not engaging" (*School Outcomes Assessment*).

As a team, choose one of the Seven Commitments to focus on in this work and align with supporting a group identified in the *School Outcomes Assessment*.

Seven Commitments Action Research Project Phases

Phase 1: Frame Your Puzzle of Practice

In this phase, you combine *Notice and Disrupt* and *Empathize and Deepen Awareness* to craft a question connected to your selected Growth Commitment and identified student group. Use student voice, classroom experiences, and equity-centered evidence to uncover underlying inequities.

Prompts to support the conversation:

- Reflect on the collective level of success with the student group identified for this action research project
- Discuss what's getting in the way of this group thriving
- What social dynamics impact the lenses of difference that this project is focused on?
- What other intersecting identities might this group have in common?
- What systems are currently in place that support efforts to engage this group?

Phase 2: Identify Action Steps

Generate bold, creative strategies that go beyond compliance as you *Ideate and Imagine Beyond Constraints*. What can we do to expand our impact at a deeper level related to this commitment and answer our Puzzle of Practice?

Actions will be:

1.

2.

3.

Phase 3: Determine Evidence

In the third phase, you draw from *Prototype and Co-Create* while identifying the types of evidence that will help you understand impact. Decide how you will measure impact and illuminate root causes. Use both experiential and schoolwide data to triangulate your findings. How will we know that we have achieved our desired goal for improvement? What will be the evidence that it is working?

Choose sources of evidence to gather the impact of the project.

1.

2.

3.

Phase 4: Take Action
Implement your actions from Phase 2. *Prototype and Co-Create* by collaboratively testing, refining, and expanding the strategies that have a positive impact. Co-design improvements with students and colleagues to deepen your practice and expand collective ownership.

Step 5: Analyze Evidence
In this final phase, you continue to *Prototype & Co-Create* to discuss and interpret the evidence. Reflect on what has shifted, what patterns are emerging, and what stories the evidence tells about your impact on the identified student group. Use results from your findings to refine your actions and co-design next steps. Consider how to scale or iterate the changes with students, colleagues, and families.

Personal Reflection

Know Self
- What evidence shows that I've been courageous in examining my own assumptions and cultural conditioning related to this student group?

- What's getting in the way of my growth?

- What support systems are available to help me stay accountable?

Know Students
- How do intersecting social dynamics affect this group's experience in my classroom?

- What do I still need to learn about the lived experiences of these students?

Know Practice
- What patterns, systems, or structures in my school support the success of this group?

- What are my next steps to deepen my practice around this principle?

Seven Commitments Student-Centered Project

"I've learned that people will forget what you said, people will forget what you did, but people will never forget how you made them feel."

– Maya Angelou

Description

In the introduction to this guidebook, Gary Howard gave credit to the "brilliant minds and caring hearts" of the scholars and leaders of the multicultural education movement, including James Banks, Carl Grant, Geneva Gay, and Sonia Nieto. Multicultural education provided a powerful counternarrative to the deficit-based, one-size-fits-all epistemologies that created barriers to success for generations of marginalized learners. Against this backdrop, esteemed researcher and author Gloria Ladson-Billings emerged as a leading voice in culturally responsive teaching. The core principles of her work, developed in the mid-1990s (Ladson-Billings, 1995), became the basis of a vast body of scholarship and practice over the past three decades. Our understanding of culturally responsive teaching has been augmented through the efforts of "next-generation" researchers and theorists. Before progressing to the engagements of this stream, we wanted to introduce several key concepts that have informed our own thinking and this body of work. A link to relevant Stewardship Commitments is also included. Our hope is that an understanding of these concepts will be useful to teams in the planning and execution of their collaborative inquiry engagements.

These ideas are woven into the Youth Empowered Stewardship (YES) Collaborative Inquiry process that grounds this guidebook. As you work through the phases of your action research project, you will be engaging in a streamlined version of the YES inquiry cycle—designed to help you notice inequities, imagine new possibilities, take bold action, and reflect on impact in partnership with students.

Note: This Action Research is designed for educators to grow critical knowledge in order to better serve a student or group of students. For a broader and deeper systemic approach to student action research, see the companion book, Youth Empowered Stewardship: A Guide to Intergenerational Partnerships.

Learning Intentions
- Design an Action Research Project to improve your practice related to a current student
- Stimulate a mutually supportive climate of shared growth among adults in your team
- Examine current resources available for student success
- Reflect on your own level of knowledge and skills to support this student's success

Student-Centered Action Research Planning
Select a current student from one of the focus groups who is not sufficiently engaged, or whom you are struggling to reach, or whom you sense is not thriving in your classroom.

Phase 1: Start with Self-Reflection on Mindsets and Experiences
Begin by examining your assumptions, cultural conditioning, and patterns of interaction with a specific student or group. Use student voice and your own reflective stance to uncover hidden inequities.

Choose from the following questions to guide your self-inquiry.
- What type of interactions have I had with this student?
- Have my interactions been primarily positive or negative?
- What have been some of the factors that have contributed to these experiences?
- What messages did I get about the lens of difference this student represents when I grew up? What are the messages in mainstream media about this group of students?
- How have these messages and experiences influenced my behaviors toward this group?

Phase 2: Name Barriers and Opportunities for Growth
Analyze what's getting in the way of student success and what existing strengths you and the student can build on. Bring in contextual data, student experiences, and professional insight to deepen awareness.
- What are the strengths, challenges, and access points for this student's success?

Phase 3: Clarify the Change You Want to See

Set an intention for what success looks like from the student's perspective and yours. Use this vision to reframe the problem and set the stage for action.

- Describe the desired state.

- What is the observable outcome I am looking for?

Phase 4: Shift Your Practice, Co-Create New Possibilities

Commit to new ways of working including changes in relationship, instruction, communication, or environment. Identify which of the Seven Commitments will guide your shift and engage students or colleagues in the design of new practices.

- What are the ways I will change my behavior and approach with this student?

- Which of the *Seven Commitments of Stewardship* will be most helpful?

Phase 5: Gather and Interpret Evidence of Impact

Collect and reflect on both qualitative and quantitative data. Look for patterns, shifts, and stories that reveal progress and next steps. Use what you learn to adapt, expand, or deepen the work.

- How will I know I have reached my goal?

- What are the metrics of success for this student?

Keep some notes and be ready to give periodic progress reports to your team in future Stewardship meetings.

Personal Reflection

Know Self
- What lessons or insights emerged for you in this process?

- What evidence is there that you've examined your assumptions with honesty and courage?

- What implicit or explicit beliefs may be getting in your way?

Know Students
- What are you learning about this student beyond academics?

- What evidence suggests you are building an authentic and effective relationship?

- What is needed?

Know Practice
- What new skills or strategies are you developing through this process?

- What support or knowledge do you still need to help this student succeed?

Stream 5: Creative Resistance

"My art is trying to figure out how I can use it to heal myself and my community."
— Theaster Gates

"Artists are not unique people, but rather, all people are unique artists."
— YES Value by W. A. Colwell and B. Howard

"I'm not self made. I'm community made, I'm family made. I'm land made. I'm ancestor made. I'm made up of everything and everyone that made me exist outside of just myself."
— Strqmul Iskwist
(Okanogan, Wanapum, Nez Perce, and Diné Indigenous, nonbinary, queer "Plateau Pop Artist")

Description

During the spring of 2021, in the midst of the COVID-19 pandemic, many of us remember joining panels, participating in Zoom visioning sessions, and engaging students in conversations about how we would like school to be different when we returned to physical classrooms. There was an incredible amount of excitement in all these conversations. Adults and students were full of ideas about changing assessment models, creating more space for building relationships, and reimagining classroom design to be more conducive to learning. More than anything, we heard people's desire for less standardized approaches, less testing, and more creativity.

When we did return to in-person learning, however, much of that excitement dissolved under the weight of "getting things back to normal," making up for "learning loss," and managing student behavior dynamics that, after months of lockdown, seemed to be more challenging to say the least—and doing all this while also having to meet the social-emotional needs of children whose families and personal lives were upended. At the same time, we also found ourselves absorbing and accommodating the language needs of families arriving from Afghanistan, Ukraine, and other conflict regions. And at the same time, educators and students found themselves at the center of a high-volume political backlash against LGBTQ students and families, against Black history, Indigenous history, Latinx history, equity and inclusion, and against teachers and public schools in general. This backlash has only amplified in recent years.

It's no wonder so many educators have become disillusioned in the past few years, many choosing to leave the profession entirely. At the same time, it is a wonder that so many of us are choosing to stay in the game and rise to meet what can seem like insurmountable, compounding challenges. Teachers deserve the honor of being recognized as essential to the nation in their commitment to children, for their ingenuity and their perseverance in the preservation of our most sacred public institution through a time of great hardship.

As a nation, we failed to learn the central lesson of the COVID-19 global pandemic: that we are all connected, our actions have impact on our neighbors and people across the globe, we are responsible for one another's health and well-being, and that freedom isn't worth anything if it's not tied to accountability, reciprocity, integrity, and honesty. Is my freedom simply my right to do harm to others, or is it tied to my civic responsibilities and my obligation to protect the freedom of others who are different from me? These are questions we explored in Stream 3.

In schools, we failed to learn another central lesson of the pandemic and distance learning—that we can change anything about the way we do business now if we want to. In a matter of months and sometimes weeks, we transferred school from classrooms to kitchens, bedrooms, living rooms, and shelter spaces. We got kids the technical resources they needed where they needed them. We fed people. We organized transportation and health care. We expanded broadband and completely reorganized how we taught classes. This is not to say that it all worked, but for many students, much of it did work. The point is that we learned we can change, and change quickly, when it's urgent. The urgency for change is still here! It didn't leave with the pandemic.

This stream of engagement is about tapping into our collective creative potential, how we imagine school functioning to meet the actual challenges in the community, and how creative expression is central to the work of an Empowered Steward. It's also an exploration of a strategy called *Creative Resistance*—a set of protocols for applying creative collaboration to address issues of power imbalance and inequity at the interpersonal and systemic levels. *Creative Resistance* was initially conceived by B. Howard and M. Born (2004) and further developed with A. Colwell (Colwell & Howard, 2018).

Empowered Stewardship has always been an arts-integrated approach to engaging with young people. If care and knowledge are the two critical components to growing stewardship, it is through the arts and creative expression that we grow both. The more the story of who we are is woven through the fabric of school life—in the murals and visual expression on the walls; in the books that we read; through music, theater, and visual art departments; in the professional learning that educators experience; in the personal storytelling and poetry that's shared in classrooms—the more we learn, the more we know, the more we care, and the less our potential for doing harm (Farrington et al., 2019). It all ties back to the lesson James

Banks taught us in the early days of the multicultural education movement: the central purpose of quality education is to *know*, to *care*, and to *act*.

In recent years, we have threaded more creative expression into professional learning for adults. We have discovered in doing so that what's good for kids is also good for adults. We have experienced, firsthand, how the use of the arts in professional learning deepens the experience for participants and elicits more strategies that can be applied in the classroom. We also have evidence that such creative expression leads to positive outcomes with respect to school climate and culture-craft as professional learning moves to the level of the heart as well as the head.

We also have learned that providing our students with access to creative expression affords tremendous benefits both within and outside of our schoolhouse doors. While the arts are often celebrated in their capacity to support social-emotional wellness, they are also critical to cultural empowerment, which is connected to academic success. The arts support increased engagement, confidence, and collaboration, which are directly tied to academic success (Bowen & Kisida, 2019). We have also seen the clear connection between academic growth and arts integration and creative expression reflected in our own case study data (Corwin Press, 2020).

Finally, when we ask educators what they want to make school work better, most teachers want less pressure, more support, and the freedom to teach to students, not to standards. When students are asked the same question, their responses generally fall into the following categories of things they want more of:

- Vibrancy
- Relevance
- Authenticity

How can we be responsive to the students' desire for school to be much more vibrant, more alive, or, as one 10th grader from Paterson, New Jersey, said, "School just needs to be more cool, more soulful, you know?" Take a moment and think about a poem, an artist, a concert, a theater event, a dance performance, or a film that stirred your soul. If we could capture that transcendent feeling in our content, our instruction, or even in the way we design our school spaces, imagine how much our students would be nourished and how much they would learn. Arts integration is the portal through which all this becomes possible. It also allows us to lean more into the artistry of teaching. From the district or building level, it's about amplifying every student's and teacher's infinite capacity for creativity by nurturing the belief that every student is an artist in their unique expression, and every teacher is an artist in their profession.

Overview of Engagement Strategies

The engagement strategies in Stream 5 invite participants to use creativity, art, and expression as tools for healing, resistance, and reimagination. These strategies expand the definition of data and action by integrating arts-based inquiry and community-rooted storytelling into collaborative inquiry cycles. They support participants in naming harm, affirming dignity, and generating bold, inclusive responses to injustice, while sustaining joy and connection. Refer to the table below for strategies that support creative resistance in pursuit of systemic change.

Layers of Engagement

Creative Resistance invites educators and students to engage in arts-based inquiry as a liberatory practice that fuels change across all levels of the system. At the personal level, individuals use artistic expression to explore identity, agency, and resistance. At the professional level, teams gather and analyze creative work as valid forms of evidence and feedback, embedding student voice into planning and practice. At the organizational level, schools adopt creative and experiential approaches to challenge dominant paradigms and expand definitions of success. These strategies support collective healing and bold reimagining of education, working to reshape societal and structural narratives through inclusive, community-rooted innovation.

Engagements that Support Collaborative Inquiry

The YES Collaborative Inquiry Process supports creative resistance by framing artistic and experiential expression as a form of equity-centered evidence. Prototypes are tested and refined not only through data but through student-led feedback, reflection, and community participation. Creative resistance serves as a liberatory strategy, uniting communities across generations in collective action to disrupt inequities, challenge oppressive narratives, and design human-centered, equitable systems that reflect the community's shared vision.

Table 6: Applying the Engagements of Stream 5 clarifies how collaborative inquiry occurs across personal, professional, and organizational dimensions. Each bullet indicates the connection to the inquiry process and where an engagement applies in the Achievement Triangle. Two stream engagements support the YES collaborative inquiry process, especially when you are designing or revising innovative ideas during the prototype and co-create phase (5) and investigate and evaluate (6) phase.

Key Engagements in Stream 5:

- **Creative Resistance – Systemic:** This provides a simple structure and set of protocols for planning action to address specific systemic inequities. (Prototype)

- **Shifting the Emotional Paradigm:** As your team gets better at running cycles of inquiry, you will undoubtedly also be getting better at having more difficult conversations about the aspects of difference and growth that tend to be controversial, political, and emotionally charged. This engagement offers up a set of personal, professional, and organizational choices that allow for richer, more nuanced, more courageous collaboration and innovation. (Notice and Disrupt, Empathy, Ideate)

Table 6: Applying the Engagements of Stream 5

Strategy	Collaborative Inquiry	Personal (Individual)	Professional (Team)	Organizational (System)
Our Roots of Stewardship: Parts 1 & 2		•		•
Creative Resistance – Interpersonal		•	•	•
Creative Resistance – Systemic	•	•	•	•
Shifting the Emotional Paradigm	•	•		•

Our Roots of Stewardship: Part 1

Description

The ocotillo (*Fouquieria splendens*), or *ocotl* in the Nahuatl language (meaning "little torch"), is an iconic plant found throughout the Southwestern desert. It grows mostly on hillside terrain and is known for its resilience to harsh, dry climates. The ocotillo has a unique relationship to the hummingbird because, in certain seasons, it might be the only source of flower nectar as it blooms throughout the year, not just in spring. This abnormal blossoming pattern allows for hummingbird migrations across the Mojave, Sonoran, and Chihuahuan deserts during the monsoon season. Most of the year, the plant is hardly exceptional. Living ocotillo appear to be dead: dry, gray-brown twisted vertical twigs, camouflaged against the landscape. But with enough rainfall, the ocotillo explode in small waxy succulent leaves and transform the basins and talus slopes into green gardens. At the end of each twisted, now green and skyward-reaching branch, red flame-shaped flowers appear overnight, perfectly shaped to accommodate the hummingbird's beak and long tongue.

We use the ocotillo as a metaphor to creatively explore the meaning of Stewardship—how we water, nurture, and feed the roots of stewardship as individuals and in community. The "blossoming" or specific outward expressions of Stewardship represent both our accomplishments that we might celebrate and the outcomes or aspirations we strive toward. Another unique aspect of the plant is its root system, which enables it to survive its often unforgiving climate. The ocotillo extends its roots out in four directions in a shallow pattern in order to seize the immediate benefit of desert rainfall and remain upright during long periods of drought and gusts of wind. For its root pattern and its ability to withstand drought, the ocotillo is a symbol of resilience and vibrancy in many cultures, from the Tohono O'odham Nation to the Hualapai and Havasupai.

Building on our metaphor, we identify the four ocotillo roots in the context of Stewardship as *courage*, *compassion*, *creativity*, and *curiosity*. These four components are sources of strength and resilience in our service of Stewardship. The first task is to imagine how these roots provide us with the strength and resilience to carry out the work of Stewardship, even when the climate seems harsh and unforgiving. What are ways in which we can nourish and water these roots? The second task is to draw or paint a picture of a plant (not necessarily an ocotillo), beginning with the four roots. The sprouts and leaves above ground are emblematic of how our stewardship shows up in the world, in our communities, and in our schools. But the work doesn't end here. Our final task is to access our own courage, compassion, creativity, and curiosity in the process of sharing, viewing, and discussing our drawings. Through active participation in this "gallery" of possibilities, we gain important insights into our inner sources of resilience as stewards and the specific outward expressions and possibilities as we grow a culture of stewardship (Colwell & Howard, 2018).

Learning Intentions

- Creatively explore the ocotillo metaphor
- Gather and document sources of strength and resiliency
- Explore, celebrate, and document stewardship actions and aspirations
- Gather and document evidence of everyday Stewardship

Figure 20: The Foundations of Your Stewardship

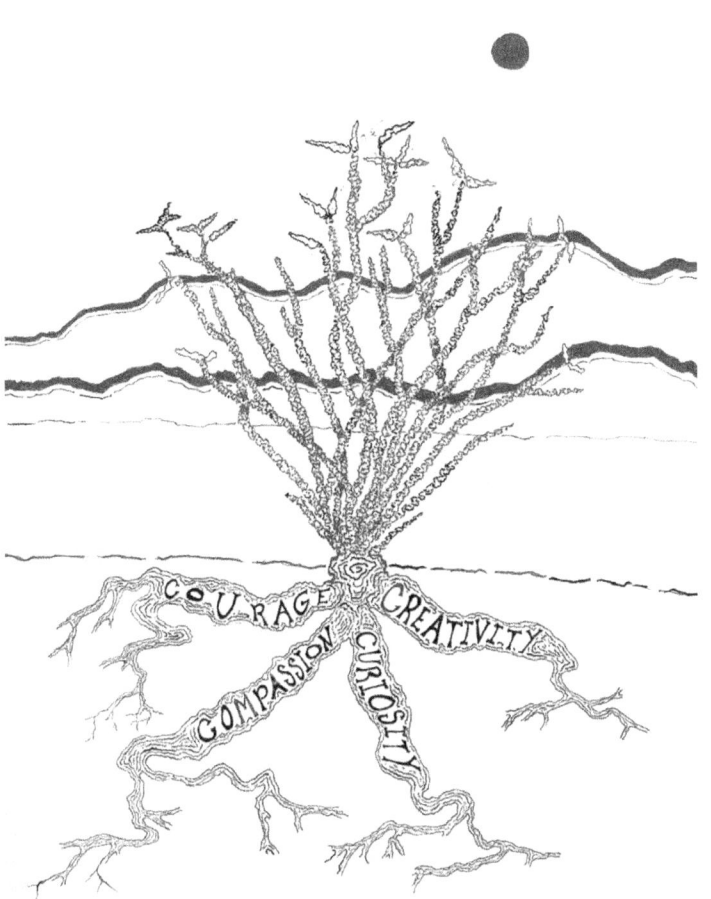

Source: Original art by Chelan Howard. Inspired by W. Colwell.

Personal Reflection

Meditate on the image. Begin to identify and take notes on the people, life experiences, influences, inspirations, and struggles that have fed or watered each of your Roots of Stewardship:

- Courage:
- Compassion:
- Creativity:
- Curiosity:

Now, imagine a plant you might draw. You may feel a connection to the ocotillo, or you may imagine something very different, from your childhood, from your yard, something iconic or native to the ecosystem where you live.

Now imagine what actions, creative expressions, relationships, aspirations, and professional accomplishments grow from your well-watered Roots of Stewardship. The branches, flowers, leaves, or needles of your plant will be labeled with the outward expressions of stewardship.

Tasks to Perform, in This Order

1. Label the roots with the 4 Cs: Courage, Compassion, Creativity, and Curiosity
2. Draw or add words and phrases that represent the nourishment or metaphorical rain that waters your roots
3. Draw your stewardship plant above ground
4. Draw or add words, phrases, or images that represent the outward expression of your stewardship

Above-Ground Creative Expression

Draw a plant above ground, above your roots, that represents how your stewardship, your care, and knowledge show up in your community. Your plant might represent something from the landscape of your childhood, something that symbolizes your purpose and vision in your work, or something that represents a plant or image from your cultural tradition. Once you have drawn your plant, write words around your plant that represent the many ways in which your stewardship shows up in the community. What actions are you taking as a steward? Who and what are you caring for? What knowledge do you provide? What actions?

Section 2: Exploring the Streams of Engagement

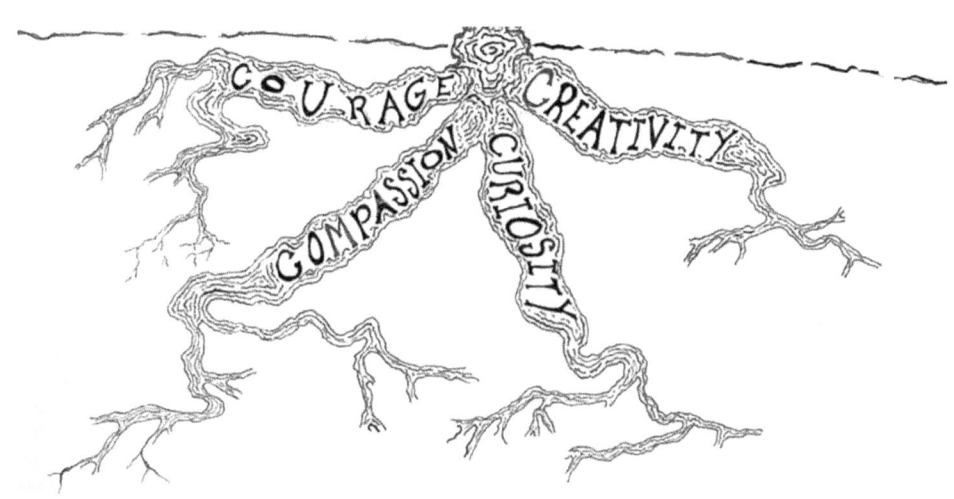

Source: Original art by Chelan Howard. Inspired by W. Colwell.

Figure 21: Roots of your Representation

Reflection and Small Group Discussion

Know Self

- Share your Roots of Stewardship artwork.
- Share your below-ground and above-ground story.
- What have you learned about yourself?
- What is the impact, or what grows for your colleagues and students from your stewardship? How are you watering other plants?

Know Students

- How might recognizing your own Roots of Stewardship help you better support your students' growth?
- What systemic barriers do you perceive being in the way of your students' roots being sufficiently watered?

Know Practice

- If equity is about nurturing a healthy educational ecosystem, where each metaphorical plant (adult/child) gets what they need to be successful on their terms, what's missing?
- How might we better water the roots and tend all our plants above ground?

Our Roots of Stewardship: Part 2

Description

Much of our American history is a story of struggle—the fight for freedom and the fundamental right to the promises of democracy: the rights of treaties and sovereignty; freedom from the tyranny of the European church and its monarchies; freedom from chattel slavery and its brutalities; the right to vote; the right to free and equal education; the freedom to speak, to believe, to love, and to pursue happiness. It can also be said that our story is a story of resilience and restoration through creativity. The arts, including music, literature, poetry, visual art, theater, and dance, are at the center of every struggle to survive and maintain dignity against a 500-year legal and cultural project of attempted erasure. The American musical lexicon holds within it the entire story of struggle—in all its complexities and multiplicities: pain, joy, and courage—to cross the visible and invisible, carefully crafted boundaries of divide and conquer that mark the darkness of our history.

It may seem trivial or simply uncomfortable at times to be invited to draw something or write a bit of poetry. But let's take a deeper look. People have been fighting and dying for equity, diversity, and inclusion for all of our history (Confessore, 2023). If our project in schools is the same as our project as a nation—to ensure that, in keeping with the ocotillo metaphor, all of us get the right amount of water, sunlight, and shade we need to thrive—then our school systems will thrive, the human ecosystem will thrive, and we will finally step into the promise of a multiracial democracy, ensuring the promise of a future for our children within it. If we're going to do all of these things, we will have to be creative!

Small Group Discussion

Consider the following statement by Jonathan Larson:

> *"The opposite of war isn't peace, it's creation."*

In what ways do you agree or disagree with this statement?
- What comfort or discomfort do you experience?
- What needs to be undone in order to establish an authentic, vibrant, and relevant creative movement in your school community?

Also consider the following statement:

> *"Artists are not unique people. All people are unique artists."*

Share your thoughts on this belief statement.

Creative Resistance – Interpersonal

"We can disagree and still love each other unless your disagreement is rooted in my oppression and denial of my humanity and right to exist."

– James Baldwin

Description

Creative Resistance is a powerful tool you can apply to difficult situations and take action for change in the moment. Identifying ways to take a stand when witnessing situations where we or others have been mistreated, these roots provide us with the strength and resilience to carry out the work of Stewardship and put pressure on systems to serve in more equitable ways. It sounds simple, but it is not.

When you are witness to, or feel you are the victim of, momentary or ongoing injustice, we all get to make a decision about how to respond. That decision may be driven to react with blind emotion, even when you have the awareness that a healthier, more productive stance is to respond with clarity.

In this engagement, we first introduce the *Justice Response Spectrum,* a powerful tool that shows the different ways we can respond to mistreatment of ourselves and others. The *Justice Response Spectrum* serves as a framework for reflecting on how our actions—or inactions—contribute to, or work against, equity and inclusion. By situating ourselves along this continuum, we develop awareness of our habitual responses and identify intentional steps for growth as stewards of justice.

Building on this foundation, we then explore the Creative Resistance Protocols. *Creative Resistance* is a choice—a choice to be creative and generative in a time when our impulse is to flee, fight, or fawn. And it is a choice to restore balance and offer dignity and possibility to those who have offended. It should also be noted that power is a factor; considering your own emotional and physical safety, as well as the ways in which power might be wielded, is critical before making the choice to employ the Creative Resistance Protocols.

Using stories from *Creative Resistance* gives you an opportunity to stop, breathe, remind yourself of the roots of your power as a steward, and plant a seed for change to grow in the future. Through this process of self-assessment and reflection using the Justice Response Spectrum, followed by practicing the Creative

Resistance Protocols, you will strengthen your capacity to respond with clarity and resilience, upholding stewardship and promoting equity in any environment.

Learning Intentions

- Describe the *Justice Response Spectrum* and analyze responses to oppression within this framework.
- Apply the Creative Resistance Protocols to real or simulated scenarios.
- Reflect on power, safety, and context in choosing resistance strategies.
- Develop actionable next steps for becoming more effective stewards and advocates for inclusion in educational (or other) settings.

Please consider your emotional and physical safety (as well as others) in a situation before engaging in a process of *Creative Resistance*. There may be dangers/threats present that require different actions to ensure safety.

Small Group Discussion

Part One - Reflect on Responses to Injustice

- Recall stories discussed in reflections from the Dynamics of Dominance exercise from Stream 3 or share another time you witnessed or experienced oppression.

Part Two - Introduce *Justice Response Spectrum*

The Justice Response Spectrum (see Figure 22), adapted from the work of Adams et al. (1997), supports self-reflection and professional growth in promoting inclusion in school ecosystems. This continuum provides a framework for educators to assess their current level of engagement and identify areas for improvement. As Empowered Stewards, examining our actions and attitudes, we can place ourselves on the spectrum, ranging from "The Co-Disruptor," actively challenging oppression and building just communities. This self-assessment allows us to recognize whether we are in stages such as "The Bystander," choosing silence over engagement, or "The Witness," recognizing injustice and questioning the current system, or "The Learner," who seeks multiple perspectives and makes internal change. As we progress through the continuum, we can set goals to move toward becoming "The Ally," who takes ownership of their impact, is open to difficult conversations about themselves, and intervenes on behalf of others. This process of self-evaluation and growth enables educators to become stronger advocates for inclusive classrooms and broader educational communities.

- Identify where our initial reactions to these situations are located on the *Justice Response Spectrum.*
- Discuss alternative reactions that would have centered your healing and truth at the moment.

Figure 22: The Justice Response Spectrum

The Bystander	The Witness	The Learner	The Ally-in-Action	The Co-Disruptor
Avoidant	Defensive	Curious	Accountable	Transformative
Supporting Oppression ➡➡➡➡➡➡➡➡➡➡➡➡➡ Confronting Oppression				

Adapted from the work of Adams et al., 1997

The Bystander

Bystanders are *avoidant*. They witness harm or exclusion but remain silent or passive. Their inaction may be rooted in fear, uncertainty, perceived lack of power, or indifference. While not intentionally harmful, the absence of a response allows injustice to persist and reinforces harmful norms.

- *Examples: Hearing a biased comment and choosing not to respond; looking away when someone is excluded or mistreated; believing "It's not my place" or "Someone else will handle it"; avoiding discomfort at the expense of others' safety.*

The Witness

Witnesses are *defensive*. They begin to recognize and feel discomfort with injustice. They may see patterns, ask questions internally, or feel a strong emotional reaction, but still hesitate to speak or act. This stage is marked by increased awareness and empathy, often a precursor to deeper engagement.

- *Examples: Feeling conflicted after observing unfair treatment; realizing how silence or complicity contributes to harm; privately discussing injustice but not raising it publicly; becoming curious about the experiences of marginalized people.*

The Learner

Learners are *curious* and engage in intentional self-reflection and seek to understand systems of oppression, privilege, and equity. They commit to personal growth and often start building skills for courageous action. This stage focuses on developing clarity, confidence, and humility.

- *Examples: Reading books, listening to podcasts, or attending training; reflecting on one's own identity and impact; practicing new language or responses for inclusive conversations; seeking feedback and learning from mistakes.*

The Ally-in-Action

Allies-in-Action are *accountable* and translate their learning into visible behaviors and consistent support for those most impacted by injustice. They disrupt harm when they see it and work in partnership to shift conditions, not to "rescue," but to redistribute power and elevate equity.

- *Examples: Calling in colleagues who use biased or exclusionary language; advocating for inclusive policies or curricular change; backing up marginalized voices in meetings and decisions; modeling anti-racist or anti-oppressive practices daily.*

The Co-Disruptor

Co-Disruptors are transformative. They collaborate with others to change structures, challenge systems, and build justice-centered cultures. They share power, amplify community wisdom, and embrace accountability. This role requires a shift from acting for others to acting with them, centering equity as collective work.

- *Examples: Co-leading equity-centered initiatives or affinity groups; designing systems that elevate marginalized voices; supporting community organizing and solidarity movements; sustaining change through shared leadership and repair.*

Part Three - *Creative Resistance* Protocol

- Revisit the incident of injustice and discuss what types of questions could have been asked that would have maintained your safety and allowed you to interrupt the situation.
- With a partner, implement the *Creative Resistance Protocol* in this situation.
- Discuss the alternate questions, responses, and expressions of truth.

Creative Resistance Protocol

⇨ Ask a Question

⇨ Listen to the Response

⇨ Speak Your Truth

Our actions are not intended to change the behaviors of the oppressor in the moment but to liberate ourselves and offer the healing gift of our truth in the moment. The growth or healing that comes from this gift may never be known to us.

Creative Resistance was developed in collaboration with M. Born.

Personal Reflection

Know Self

- What patterns do you notice in how you tend to respond to moments of injustice or exclusion?

- How did practicing the Creative Resistance Protocol shift your thinking or offer new possibilities for action?

Know Students

- How might your students experience moments of injustice, and how can the Justice Response Spectrum help you better understand their needs and behaviors?

- In what ways could modeling Creative Resistance support students' development of voice, agency, and resilience?

Know Practice

- How might you use the Justice Response Spectrum to reflect on and guide your own professional decisions and team conversations?

- How could you embed the Creative Resistance Protocol into classroom or schoolwide routines to foster safety, dignity, and inclusion?

Creative Resistance – Systemic

> *"We delight in the beauty of the butterfly, but rarely admit the changes it has gone through to achieve that beauty."*
>
> – Maya Angelou

Description

We talked in Stream 3 about ways the dynamics of dominance show up in our everyday relationships—the Assumption of Rightness, the Luxury of Ignorance, and the Legacy of Privilege. We also talked about how they show up systemically in our schools, prisons, neighborhoods, in health care and banking systems, and in society in general (see *Privilege and Power Assessment*). We have shared how *Creative Resistance* can be put into play in the moment when we have been mistreated or we have witnessed the mistreatment of others. *Creative Resistance* is a term we use to talk about how we can respond to greater systemic forms of injustice. The process remains the same. It's about *responding* rather than *reacting* with blind emotion. It's an opportunity to release ourselves and others from the full weight of an unjust system, and it's about planting seeds for change.

The difference between *Creative Resistance* in interpersonal situations and *Creative Resistance* in response to systemic problems is that we don't respond so much in the moment but *take action over time*, and that we work *together* rather than on our own!

For Systemic *Creative Resistance*, we have adapted the process in the following way:
- Ask critical questions
- Listen to different voices
- Take action together over time

Learning Intentions
- Understand the *Creative Resistance Protocols* (CRPs)
- Apply the CRPs to scenarios from Stream 3 storytelling
- Describe classroom applications of *Creative Resistance*

Small Group Discussion

Ask Critical Questions

Remember: Everyone's voice needs to be heard! If one or two people are taking up all the airwaves, you are not getting the wisdom from your group. This is a democratic space, keep the circle. There is no one leader. One person will need to record your answers and ideas. Two people will be chosen to share your plan with the larger group.

Challenge: The problem or scenario you choose to address through *Creative Resistance* must include some significant social or environmental impact in your community. It must also be perceived as having a solution with a reasonable pathway toward success. This means that people care about it enough to put their energy toward the issue.

- What is the issue?

- How is the issue momentary and/or ongoing?

- Who are the people with power in this situation? Who feels powerless?

Listen to Different Voices

Although we are not always able to hear from all people affected in a real-world scenario, let's challenge ourselves to imagine what we might hear. Let's include the different people involved, their perspectives, and consider multiple potential responses.

- What story or stories might you hear from people who hold power in this situation?

- What stories might you hear from people who feel powerless in this situation?

- What do you know about the history leading up to the situation?

Take Actions Together Over Time

- Who are your allies or people who can support you?

- How will you go about organizing people to support you in your efforts?

- How will you create a brave and inspired space for planning?

- What is the *truth* you want to speak?

- How do you want to say it? Who is your audience?

- What *collective action* do you want to take?

- When and where will you do this?

Systemic Creative Resistance developed in collaboration with M. Born

Shifting the Emotional Paradigm

Description

This engagement strategy can be used anytime in the Stewardship process when you or your facilitators decide it would be most helpful. Any discussion of the Stream 3 content, dominance, marginalization, privilege, power, and oppression, can often take us out of our comfort zones, touching areas of personal pain or challenging us to move beyond our familiar paradigms and personal perceptions of what is real and true. In this engagement strategy, we address several of what we call the "Emotions That Hurt," including fear, denial, hostility, blame, shame, and guilt—emotions that can surface as individuals and groups work with the movement from Social Dominance to Justice for All—emotions that are real and must be acknowledged and dealt with on the journey toward deep and authentic conversation and transformative action.

When difficult emotions do emerge while you are dealing with these complex issues, it is important not to leave people stuck in that place; rather, talk explicitly about these feelings that can get in the way of authentic communication and impede real growth and understanding. Sometimes, merely by acknowledging the legitimacy of these feelings, we can open the way to deeper learning. It is also important to point out that if we are *not* experiencing some discomfort dealing with these topics, we are probably not having a real conversation.

In this engagement strategy, we also address positive options to each of these challenging emotions, options that we refer to as "Responses That Heal"—including humility, honesty, empathy, advocacy, and action. You and your colleagues and students can discuss which of the "Emotions That Hurt" you may have experienced or witnessed during your work together, and what you consider to be some responses that can lead to positive movement and personal growth.

Learning Intentions

- Address the emotional component of transformative change
- Identify those emotions that can get in the way of personal growth and organizational change
- Identify and describe healing alternatives for addressing difficult emotions
- Cultivate emotional resilience within Stewardship communities

Discussion Guide

Shifting the Emotional Paradigm

EMOTIONS THAT HURT	RESPONSES THAT HEAL
Fear	Humility
Denial	Honesty
Hostility	Empathy
Blame	Advocacy
Shame/Guilt	Action

Small Group Discussion:

1. Which of these Emotions That Hurt have you seen or sensed being present in your Stewardship interactions with your colleagues or students?

2. Share an experience where you were able to shift your own emotional frame from *Hurt* to *Heal*.

3. What would you want to add to the Emotions That Hurt list or the Responses That Heal list?

4. What has to happen for us to move from the emotions that shut down conversations to the responses that open new possibilities for connection and growth? What are the preconditions for this kind of transformation?

Further Considerations

- Where would anger go on these lists of emotions? Can anger be both an Emotion That Hurts and a Response That Heals? In what ways?

- It would be helpful to revisit the *Climate Assessment* engagement strategy you experienced in Stream 1, and connect that discussion with the work you are doing here with *Shifting the Emotional Paradigm*. How do the Emotions That Hurt and the Responses That Heal play into the presence or absence of trust? What shifts have you seen among your colleagues and students as you have engaged these topics?

Personal Reflection

Know Self

- How do you personally move from emotions that hurt toward responses that heal?

- What is your overall reaction to the discussion of emotions presented here?

- How have you felt about the *Shifting the Emotional Paradigm* conversations you have had with your colleagues and/or students?

- What Emotions That Hurt would you add to the included list?

- What Responses That Heal would you add?

- Which of these emotions have you experienced in the process of conversations with your colleagues? Which of the Responses That Heal have you been able to express?

Know Students
- How could you help students name and navigate difficult emotions in learning spaces?

Know Practice
- To what extent have you and your colleagues and students been willing and able to have honest and real conversations about the emotional component of your Stewardship work?

  ⇨ What seems to be working?

  ⇨ What is getting in the way?

- What are you presently doing, or what could you do, to help shift the emotional tone of your community of colleagues and students toward greater trust and healing?

- What practices could support a more emotionally resilient and trusting school culture?

The Desert Monsoon Model: Closing the Gap Between Student Voice and Student Agency

As a cautionary note, in our work, it often takes a year to facilitate the full Desert Monsoon Model and provide district administrators with a thorough, creative documentation of youth and adult perspectives on all five aspects. We have heard educators express admiration and astonishment for the level at which young people are able to articulate their experience and imagine the possibility of growth and change. We have also heard their astonishment over the abuse and mistreatment students experience in school settings, as well as admiration for those same students' capacity for hope and creative ideas. We've also seen the whole record get filed away and the action plans that result get buried in the complexity of the following school year.

The five monsoon conversations and record-keeping must only be the beginning of a much larger, creative, courageous, intergenerational project. By year two in the implementation of this work, Youth Stewardship Ambassadors must be seated at decision-making tables at the building and district levels. They should be included in equity team efforts. They should be a part of your collaborative inquiry process. They should be the ones who identify priorities within the recorded issues in the drought aspect. It's adults who can support the mapping from those specific priorities, through the corresponding aspects of hope and vision, toward specific actionable moves. The harder work, then, is to adjust adult ways of being and behaviors in order to manifest the change that students envision. That's where the opportunities for growth outlined in these previous chapters are critical. Every engagement strategy in this book is an opportunity to grow personal and collective capacity toward nurturing a culture of empowered Stewardship and dynamics of shared power in your school community.

The Desert Monsoon process is a culminating activity. Its impact will be directly and greatly enhanced if the educators and students who are engaging in the process have previously done much of the Stewardship work explored throughout this guidebook. There are some specific engagements that will undoubtedly make the Desert Monsoon process more productive:

- *Personal Growth Project*
- Deep exploration of the *Achievement Triangle*
- Understanding and experience with the *Seven Commitments for Stewardship Practice*
- *Creative Resistance – Systemic* (This provides a roadmap for action planning based on the Desert Monsoon Model.)

A much more detailed outline of the student-led Monsoon inquiry and action planning process can be found in the Youth Empowered Stewardship: Creating Intergenerational Partnership Together.

The Desert Monsoon Model

Model originally conceived by W. Colwell and co-developed by W. Colwell & B. Howard. A much more detailed outline of the student-led Monsoon inquiry and action planning process can be found in the companion book, Youth Empowered Stewardship: Creating Intergenerational Partnership Together.

Description

In the deserts of the American Southwest and Northern Mexico, the monsoon season typically arrives in late Summer and brings much-needed rainfall to the dry landscape. The pattern of late summer storm systems originating in the Gulf of Mexico and building as they travel north over the land remains somewhat predictable. Still, it has become much more erratic and violent over the last decade, given that climate shifts have altered the centuries-old pattern of late July and August precipitation. The metaphor of a monsoon allows us to explore Creative Resistance in a meaningful, creative, and land-based way.

As a reminder, Creative Resistance is the deliberate, generative choice to respond to injustice, whether interpersonal or systemic, not with reactivity or withdrawal, but with creativity, compassion, and clarity. Rooted in the values of Stewardship, it involves engaging in reflective action that restores dignity, reclaims agency, and plants seeds for future transformation.

Rather than fleeing, fighting, or fawning when faced with harm, Creative Resistance invites individuals and communities to pause, reflect using tools like the Justice Response Spectrum, and practice protocols that build capacity for long-term equity work. In interpersonal situations, it provides a way to respond constructively in the moment. In systemic contexts, it calls for sustained, collective action over time.

Creative Resistance is a liberatory practice—one that transforms hurt into healing, blame into responsibility, and isolation into solidarity. It uses arts-based, experiential, and human-centered methodologies to reimagine schools and communities as places where justice and joy coexist.

In keeping with our Stewardship intention to connect visual models and metaphors to actual ecosystems, places, and people, the Desert Monsoon Model allows us to explore the work of transforming how we do school better in a way that maintains authenticity, vibrancy, and relevance—connections to real places and people. We have seen this model creatively modified for cultural and natural environments beyond the arid Southwest, making it more relevant to real communities where it's being applied. There are multiple ways to engage the Desert Monsoon Model, and the possibilities for creative innovation are endless.

In general, the Desert Monsoon Model supports an ongoing intergenerational conversation about understanding the challenges we face and how to do better together. The structure itself allows for a kind of liberation from a problem-solution binary mindset when discussing change, improvement, and impact, enabling a more three-dimensional approach. It's a set of five conversations that should take place over time (we often engage the Desert Monsoon Model over the course of one school year). Each conversation allows for a gathering of perspectives from across the school community, and each conversation is connected metaphorically to five aspects of a desert monsoon. So let's imagine these aspects for a moment.

The late summer monsoon in the arid Southwest is always preceded by drought, a period of time when much of the life in the desert appears to be dead, the landscape is brown, springs dry up, and plants and animals seek shelter from the oppressive heat. In the late summer, in the afternoon, storm systems flow north from the Gulf over the Coahuila, Chihuahua, Sonora, and high deserts. They bring much-needed cloud cover and shade, and the promise of rain. If we are lucky, those cumulus cloud systems build and may produce thunder and lightning, and even more promise of rain. And finally, the rain may fall and replenish the land, sometimes light and gentle, and other times a torrent of flash flooding, producing immediate changes to the landscape. Oftentimes, after a monsoon storm, a rainbow might appear, and always, with enough water, the desert becomes green again and full of life.

The Discussion

There are multiple formats for these Monsoon discussions. One way we've engaged them is in a "fishbowl" format, where there is an inner circle of speakers and an outer circle of listeners. We've structured it as an ongoing dialogue with youth advisories. We've invited families and community members to join in and contribute. The critical piece is to document the conversation so that you have a record of perspectives across the diversity in your classroom, workgroup, or community, and notes related to each aspect of the Desert Monsoon.

The knowledge acquired in the Drought and Gathering Clouds aspects can then be introduced into the qualitative/ empathy data sets you are gathering in your inquiry process. The Thunder/ Lightning knowledge can be introduced into your ideation process. The Rain aspect can be included in the action planning section of your inquiry.

As a cautionary note, in our work, it often takes a year to facilitate the complete Desert Monsoon Model and provide district administrators with a thorough, creative documentation of youth and adult perspectives on all five aspects. We have heard educators express admiration and astonishment for the level at which young people can articulate their experience and imagine the possibility of growth and change. We have also heard their astonishment over the abuse and mistreatment students experience in school settings, as well as admiration for those same students' capacity for hope and creative ideas. We've also seen the whole record get filed away, and the action plans that result get buried in the complexity of the following school year.

The five monsoon conversations and record-keeping must only be the beginning of a much larger, creative, courageous, intergenerational project. By year two in the implementation of this work, Youth Stewardship Ambassadors must be seated at decision-making tables at the building and district levels. They should be included in equity team efforts. They should be a part of your collaborative inquiry process. They should be the ones who identify priorities within the recorded issues in the drought aspect. It's adults who can support the mapping from those specific priorities, through the corresponding aspects of hope and vision, toward specific actionable moves. The more complex work, then, is to adjust adult ways of being and behaviors in order to manifest the change that students envision. That's where the opportunities for growth outlined in these previous chapters are critical. Every engagement strategy in this book is an opportunity to grow personal and collective capacity toward nurturing a culture of empowered Stewardship and the dynamics of shared power in your school community.

The Desert Monsoon process is a culminating activity. Its impact will be directly and greatly enhanced if the educators and students engaging in the process have previously undertaken much of the Stewardship work explored throughout this guidebook. Some specific engagements will undoubtedly make the Desert Monsoon process more productive:

Personal Growth Project
- Deep exploration of the Achievement Triangle

- Understanding and experience with the *Seven Commitments for Stewardship Practice*

- *Creative Resistance – Systemic* (This provides a roadmap for action planning based on the Desert Monsoon Model.)

The Five Aspects of a Desert Monsoon

Here are the five aspects. Each one is followed by an example of a creative record of those conversations created in a school district in Washington State (see Figures 23–27).

	**The Drought:** This is a discussion of what is lacking. Whose needs are not being met? Whose voices are not being heard? Whose voices are dominating? Which groups of people in the school community are experiencing disempowerment? What resources are missing?

Figure 23: Intergenerational Example of The Drought

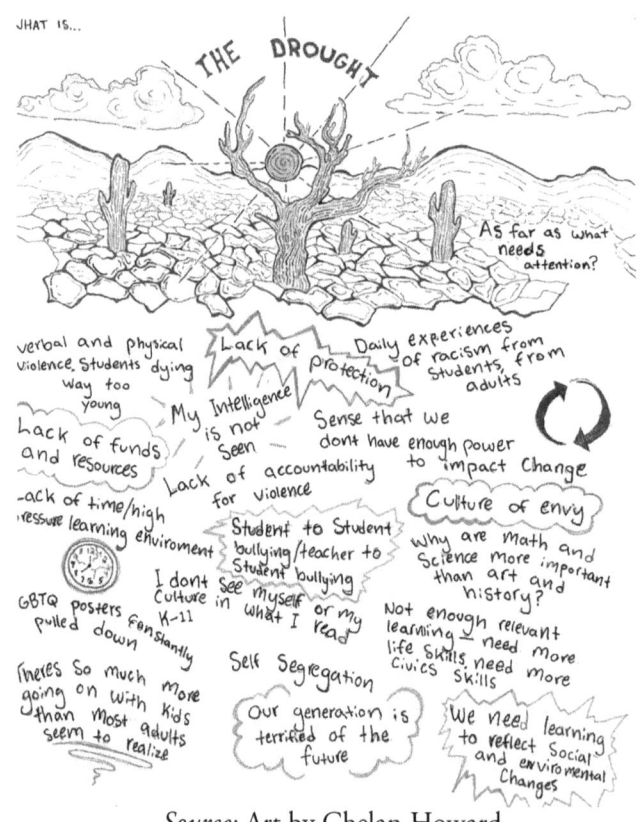

Source: Art by Chelan Howard

218

Section 2: Exploring the Streams of Engagement

| | **The Gathering of Clouds:** This is a discussion about hope. What events or realities give us hope toward qualitative and quantitative change? |

Figure 24: Intergenerational Example of The Clouds in the Sky

Source: Art by Chelan Howard

	Thunder and Lightning: This is a discussion about unlimited ideas for change. If there were no barriers, what structural and systemic changes would we like to manifest? What is the shape of our collective "Us-topia"?

Figure 25: Intergenerational Example of Thunder and Lightning

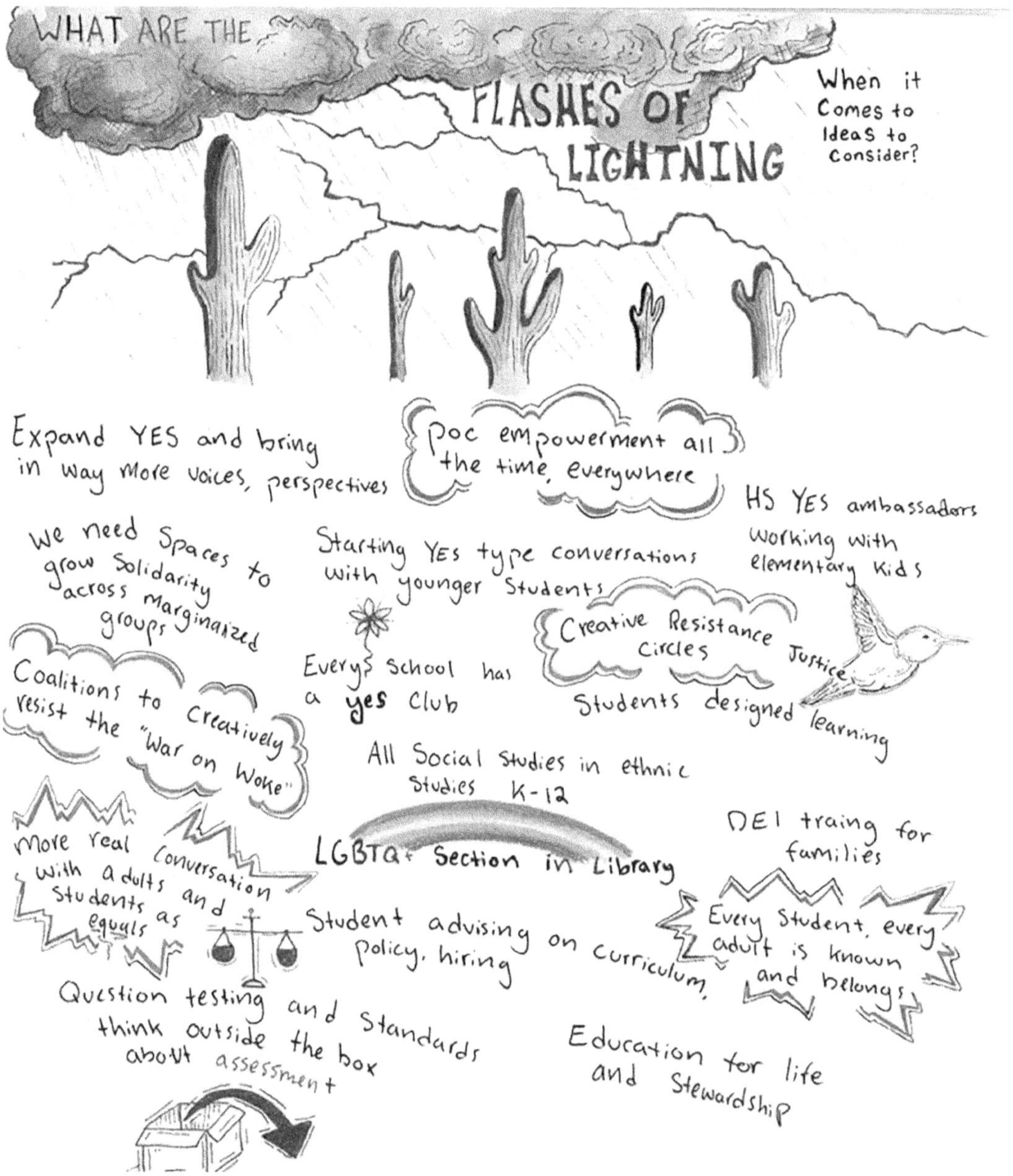

Source: Art by Chelan Howard

Section 2: Exploring the Streams of Engagement

 Rain: This is the action we plan to take based on our understanding of what is lacking or missing, how we are hopeful, our understanding of unlimited possibility, and the refreshing and real actionable change that we envision.

Figure 26: Intergenerational Example of Rain

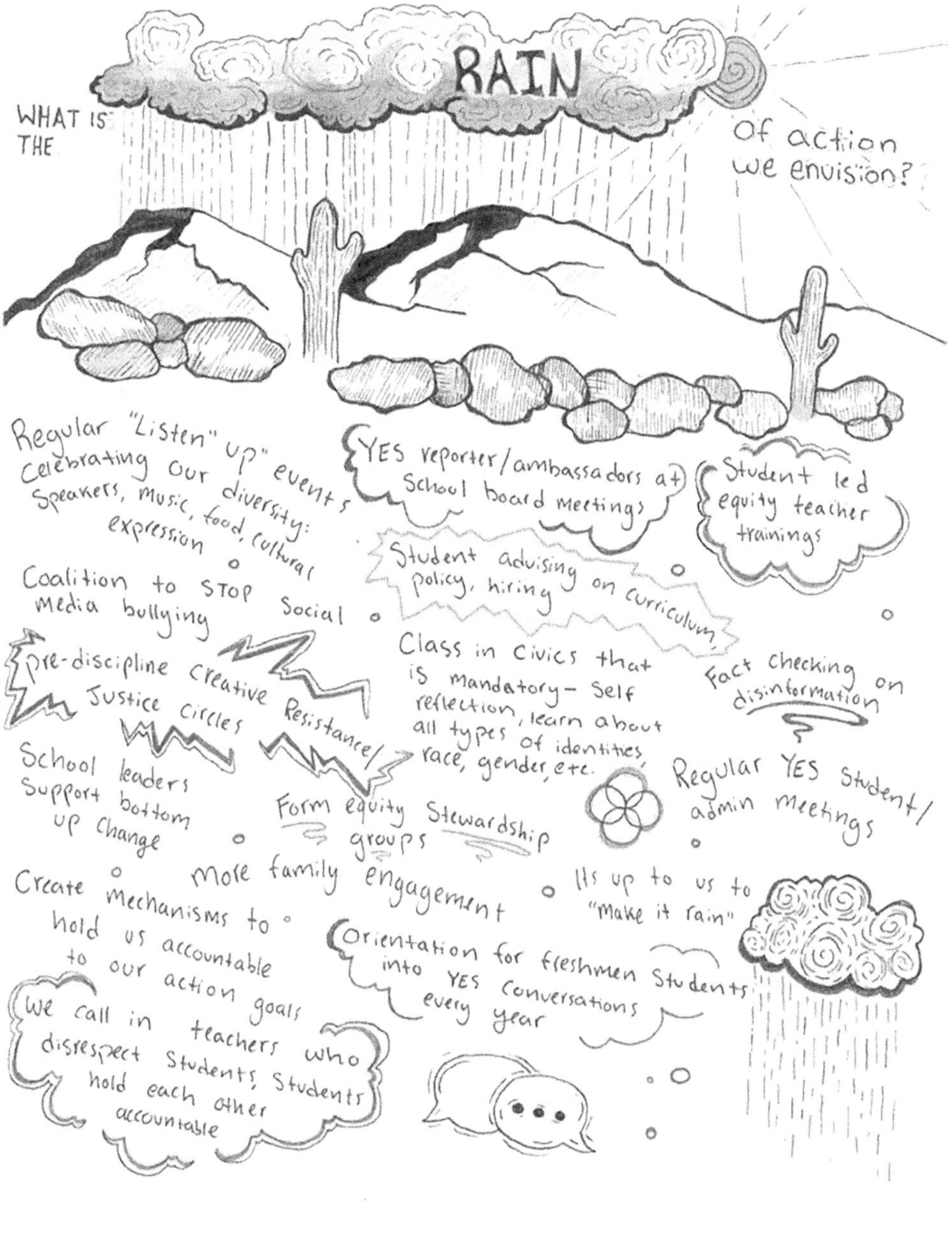

Source: Art by Chelan Howard

> **The Rainbow:** This is a discussion about ways of being, not just what we do, but how we are: the ways of being that we choose to inhabit and the impact of sustainable shifts toward growing a culture of Stewardship.

Figure 27: Intergenerational Example of Rainbow

Desert Monsoon Model was developed in collaboration with W.A. Colwell

The Rainbow: A Note for Stewards

If there is a central lesson we have learned as a team of colleagues, friends, family, and coauthors in this work over the past 20 to 50 years, it is that *what* we do is important, but *how* we do it is even more vital. Changing ourselves is difficult; changing other people is nearly impossible; changing systems is even harder. But we are also surrounded by evidence of real, meaningful, and measurable change happening all the time. If we continue to work at it, we will have personal, professional, organizational, and, hopefully, societal impact. Change is the one thing we can rely on—we will grow, our systems will grow, if we do the work. As educators, leaders, and students, we may not have the ability or the power to predict the exact shape or breadth of our impact, but we will make change if we intend it, and we will be more effective if we are willing to change ourselves before we ask it of others. It's the listening piece of Creative Resistance that is often missing.

This is why we love the fact that we are ending this conversation with the fifth aspect of the Desert Monsoon: The Rainbow. This is the place in the conversation where we choose and grow how to be with ourselves, how to be with one another as professionals, and how to be in community. This is our opportunity to explore and wrestle with the most critical questions facing us at this particular time in history. This is where we learn to dance with the rhythm and light of the rainbow—through reflection, refraction, and dispersion.

- **Reflection:** (*In Lak'ech*) What is our capacity to see ourselves reflected in another person who is different from us? To see ourselves reflected in nature? What is our capacity for reciprocity?

- **Refraction:** What is our capacity to shift our thinking and shift our heart based on what we learn from listening to someone different from us? From the community? From the natural world?

- **Dispersion:** How do we make sure that the lessons of light, lessons of the rainbow, lessons of ways of being, of reflection and refraction, don't stay isolated in the interpersonal or classroom space, but can expand across the entire community?

In Closing

While the image of a rainbow stands alone as an aspect of nature—as a common aftereffect of an actual monsoon rain in the desert, and as a miracle that we will all hopefully experience at least one more time in our lives—the rainbow is also a symbol and a metaphor. It has many meanings in many traditions across the globe, but there are also threads of meaning that rhyme, especially across a multitude of Indigenous perspectives. In Lakota and Diné tradition, the rainbow represents transcendence or the pathway between worlds. Generally, across cultures, the rainbow holds meaning as a bridge between the physical and spiritual worlds. It represents harmony, balance, beauty, imagination, and transformation.

Think of Jesse Jackson's Rainbow Coalition in the 1980s, an idea originally framed by Fred Hampton that aimed to bring people together from multiple racial backgrounds and advance the realization of a true American multiracial democracy.

And of course, the rainbow is a flag of pride that represents the struggle, the survival, and triumph for the Queer community. The rainbow flag is a symbol that represents people who are under attack in communities, in schools, and in states across the nation, through physical and rhetorical violence, attempts at erasure, misinformation, disinformation, book bans, and media malpractice. We choose to close this learning journey here with you in this way, in solidarity and in allyship with the "People of the Rainbow." This includes all our Two-Spirited warriors, all our precious Queer folk. Without you, we will never truly know the Roots of Stewardship. Without you, we don't truly know Courage, we don't know Compassion, we don't know Creativity or Curiosity.

For me (Benjie) personally, and for us as a team of coauthors, the rainbow ultimately represents hope; not fluffy unicorn hope, but rather the hard-earned, well-informed, light after the darkness reminder of the miracle of life on Earth, Rainbow Coalition kind of hope—the kind of hope that emphasizes the *All* in Freedom, Justice and Equality for *All*. The kind of audacious and courageous hope that has carried us into the light of multiple emancipations and reconstructions throughout our history, and helped us survive through the darkness of backlash, the revisionist redemptions that inevitably follow every historic moment when we get closer to the promise of Democracy. I recently had a conversation about hope with Yared, a student in Paterson, New Jersey. He said that he used to think the concept of hope was "kind of cheesy," that to be hopeful, people had to be ignorant of the real struggles folks in his community are experiencing.

But he had recently changed his mind. He felt like his friends and other young people in his school were less concerned with what they were going to do for a living in the future and more concerned about whether they would have a future. He said that when people in power are actively betting against the future, hope is a different kind of thing. He said, "Hope is a blue-collar job. Just like my mom, you just gotta get up every morning and go to work."

We sincerely hope that you have grown in this professional learning journey, that you feel in some way hopeful, that your role as an Empowered Steward in partnership with your colleagues and students is in some way a coming home to why you chose this profession in the first place. These aspects of light, *reflection, refraction, and dispersion* are learned skills, but they are also natural ways of being for most of us. Our future and the future of our children are in our hands as educators. We got this.

Just like moms, let's get up this morning and go to work.

Glossary

Achievement Triangle – A foundational framework in the YES Collaborative Inquiry process that guides culturally responsive practice through three interrelated domains: knowledge of self, knowledge of students, and knowledge of practice.

Affirmation Before Reformation – A principle of Empowered Stewardship that prioritizes affirming the humanity and strengths of educators before seeking changes in their practice.

Agency – The capacity of students or educators to take intentional action, make choices, and direct their own learning or professional growth.

Alignment (Four A's) – Ensuring Stewardship work connects to a school or district's mission, vision, and ongoing equity efforts, avoiding duplication or isolation.

Amplifying Voice – Centering and elevating the experiences and perspectives of students, families, and communities, particularly those historically marginalized.

Arts-Based Engagement – The use of music, visual art, movement, and other creative forms as core elements of professional learning and student inquiry to deepen understanding, foster connection, and inspire action.

Asset-Based – An approach that focuses on the strengths, skills, and cultural wealth of students, educators, and communities, rather than framing them through deficits or gaps.

Beloved Community – A vision of a society based on justice, equity, and love for one's fellow human beings, amplified by Dr. Martin Luther King Jr., and used in educational contexts to describe inclusive school communities.

Bridge of Practice – A metaphor used in Empowered Stewardship to describe the connection between professional learning and classroom practice, ensuring that 7 Stewardship Commitments are translated into daily actions.

Capacity Building – The process of developing the knowledge, skills, and dispositions needed by educators, students, and communities to lead and sustain equity-driven change.

Collective Care – A shared commitment among educators, students, and community members to support each other's well-being as an integral part of achieving equity.

Collective Efficacy – The shared belief among a group of educators that they have the ability to positively impact student outcomes through joint effort.

Community Agreements – Mutually developed norms that set expectations for respectful communication, collaboration, and accountability in learning spaces.

Creative Resistance – The intentional choice to respond to injustice with creativity, clarity, and care, transforming harmful moments into opportunities for healing and change.

Cultural Competence – The ability to understand, value, and effectively interact with people across cultures, adapting practices to meet diverse needs.

Cultural Humility – A lifelong process of self-reflection and learning about other cultures, recognizing one's own biases, and engaging respectfully across differences.

Culturally Responsive Pedagogy – An instructional approach that integrates students' cultural backgrounds, experiences, and perspectives into teaching to enhance engagement and achievement.

Define & Reframe – A phase of the YES Collaborative Inquiry Process where teams clearly articulate their "puzzle of practice" and reframe challenges to address root causes rather than symptoms.

Democratic Education – An educational philosophy that instills values such as freedom, equality, and justice through shared decision-making and active civic participation.

Empathize & Deepen Awareness – A phase of the YES Collaborative Inquiry Process in which teams gather stories, lived experiences, and qualitative data—especially from those most impacted by inequity—to uncover root causes and recognize cultural assets.

Equity – Providing each learner with the resources and support they need to succeed, acknowledging and addressing systemic barriers and starting point differences.

Evaluate & Sustain – A phase of the YES Collaborative Inquiry Process focused on measuring impact, celebrating successes, refining actions, and embedding effective practices into the school's culture for long-term change.

Four A's – A reflective leadership tool—Alignment, Accountability, Assessment, and Advocacy—used to assess progress and guide implementation of Stewardship work.

Front Porch Commitments – The first three of the Seven Stewardship Commitments, focusing on affirming cultural identities, building respectful relationships, and creating welcoming, culturally relevant environments.

House of Learning – A metaphorical framework in Empowered Stewardship that visualizes the components of an equitable school culture as structural elements of a house, emphasizing that all parts, foundation, walls, and roof, must be strong and connected for learning to thrive.

Human-Centered Design – A creative problem-solving approach that centers the needs, experiences, and perspectives of people most affected by a challenge.

Ideate & Imagine Beyond Constraints – A phase of the YES Collaborative Inquiry Process in which teams brainstorm bold, justice-centered possibilities that disrupt "business as usual" and honor learner voice, identity, and agency.

Impact Teams – A collaborative inquiry model that advances instructional excellence and learner agency through evidence-based reflection and decision-making.

Intergenerational Partnerships – Collaborations between people of different age groups—especially youth and adults—to share leadership, knowledge, and responsibility in shaping learning environments.

Justice-Driven – Approaches and actions in education aimed at dismantling systemic inequities and advancing fairness and inclusion for all learners.

Layers of Engagement – A framework emphasizing transformation across personal, professional, organizational, and societal layers for sustainable equity and excellence.

Liberatory Design – A design framework that integrates empathy, iteration, and co-creation to dismantle inequities and shift power dynamics toward justice.

Liberatory Pedagogies – Teaching practices designed to free learners from systems of oppression, often incorporating critical thinking, reflection, and student voice.

Multilingual Learners (MLs) – Students who are in the process of acquiring proficiency in more than one language, often requiring specialized instructional support.

Neuroplasticity – The brain's ability to reorganize itself by forming new neural connections throughout life, allowing for learning and adaptation.

Notice & Disrupt – A phase of the YES Collaborative Inquiry Process that invites teams to identify inequities in school structures and practices, challenge dominant narratives, and disrupt the assumptions that sustain them.

Organizational Layer – The level of the Layers of Engagement framework that focuses on schoolwide systems, policies, and structures impacting equity and excellence.

Personal Layer – The level of the Layers of Engagement framework that focuses on individual beliefs, mindsets, and practices as they relate to equity and stewardship.

Practice Side of the Achievement Triangle – The instructional and leadership practices that result from self-awareness and knowledge of students, applied to create equitable learning environments.

Prototype & Co-Create – A phase of the YES Collaborative Inquiry Process where ideas are turned into action through collaborative experimentation, testing, and iteration with students and families.

Section 2: Exploring the Streams of Engagement

Puzzle of Practice – A specific challenge or problem in teaching and learning identified through collaborative inquiry for deeper investigation and solution design.

Radical Welcoming – An intentional practice of creating spaces where every individual, particularly those historically excluded, is actively invited, valued, and affirmed.

Seven Stewardship Commitments – A set of core practices defining what it means to be a steward in an equity-centered school, guiding daily actions and interactions.

Societal/Structural Layer – The level of the Layers of Engagement framework that addresses larger systemic and cultural forces influencing education.

Stewardship – The act of caring for and taking responsibility for the well-being of people, communities, and the environment through equity-centered relationships and action.

Transformative Relationship-Building – Developing authentic, trust-filled relationships that challenge inequities and serve as the foundation for collective action.

Youth Empowered Stewardship (YES) – An arts-based, equity-focused framework engaging students, educators, and communities as co-creators of school culture and systemic transformation.

YES Collaborative Inquiry Process – A cyclical, liberatory model in which students and adults co-design equitable learning environments through iterative reflection and action.

Appendices

Additional downloadable tools, extended examples, videos, and printable resources are available on the Mimi & Todd Press website.

Three appendices in particular provide practical tools to support the implementation of the YES Collaborative Inquiry Process and YES Engagement Strategies in your district, school, or classroom. You will find a blank template to guide your own inquiry cycles, a collection of "snapshots" offering abbreviated examples from real teams in varied settings, and a table clarifying which strategies are most often used with specific phases in the inquiry process.

- Appendix A: YES Collaborative Inquiry Process Template
- Appendix B: Collaborative Inquiry "Snapshots"
- Appendix C: Recommended Engagement Strategies for Each Phase of Inquiry

Use the QR code below to access the full library of companion materials and check back as the authors continue to share what they and their partners in schools develop.

Acknowledgements

From Benjie and Gary—We want to acknowledge the people who have contributed their creativity, ideas, and support in the construction of this guide. To Wade Antonio Colwell, whose music, artistry, and leadership helped shape our work, and who co-created with Benjie the *In My One Beat, Ocotillo* and Monsoon Engagement strategies included in this guidebook. To Maketa Born, who co-founded the work with Benjie, and whose creative expression and vision helped launch the intergenerational aspect of this work. To Naomi Kalom, whose patience, listening, and perspective have been invaluable. To Reya Born, whose thinking and writing on issues of race-based health care disparities have strengthened our Stream 3 work. To Chelan Howard, who has deepened the impact of this project through her visual art. To Dan Alpert, whose brilliance and wisdom as a collaborator and editor have shaped this book. To Dr. Lotus Linton Howard, who has always been our role model for transformative multicultural teaching. This list mirrors what you will find within the descriptions of each stream in Section 2 and even in the narrative inquiry example from Part 4 of Section 1 in this book, but is meant to help you make determinations about which engagement strategies you might use in different phases of inquiry.

From Patricia—I want to express deep gratitude to my childhood friends from High Point Elementary School. You inspired my earliest dreams of becoming a teacher and embedded in me the core belief that every student deserves to see themselves—truly and fully—in their classroom experiences. You showed me, from the very start, that representation matters. To my son, Xahil: Your authenticity, vulnerability, and lived experience as a young man of color continually open my eyes to what equity and justice look like in action. Thank you for being my greatest teacher. I am also profoundly thankful for my colleagues and students at Highline College. Your strength and commitment keep me grounded, reminding me each day that nurturing educators to challenge and disrupt systems of educational oppression is our shared responsibility. Eliminating barriers to student success is not optional, but the essential work of every educator.

To The Core Collaborative and Mimi and Todd Press—We have all published works in the past, but never with the level of care and intention we experienced with our current partners in this work. To Katie Smith, Leah Tierney, and Tony Francoeur – your hospitality, generosity, and structural support not only helped make this book happen, but also made it possible for us to put new frameworks and strategies into play in school districts where the new Empowered Stewardship approach could be tested as we put pen to paper. To Sarah Stevens, Dr. Paul Bloomberg, and Isaac Wells, this book came together at a unique time in the U.S. and the world. As history unfolded or unraveled around us, the book evolved in order to meet the very real and rapid challenges emerging in public education in real time. From the intensive retreat in Palm Springs to the countless 12-14 hour days that you all committed to getting this project across the finish line—for your love, for your wisdom, for your genuine belief in the project, and for your forged-in-fire true commitment to collaboration—we are grateful.

References

Adams, M., Bell, L., & Griffin, P. (1997). *Teaching for diversity and social justice: A sourcebook*. Routledge.

Acosta, M. M., & Mir, A. (2012). Charting a path toward equitable representation of Latino students in higher education. *Journal of Hispanic Higher Education*, 11(4), 359-371.

Baldwin, J. (1955). *Notes of a native son*. Beacon Press.

Banks, J. A. (2016). *Cultural diversity and education: Foundations, curriculum, and teaching*. Routledge.

Bertrand, M., & Rodela, K. C. (2018). A framework for rethinking educational leadership in the margins: Implications for social justice leadership preparation. *Journal of Research on Leadership Education*, 13(1), 10-37.

Betancourt, J. R., Green, A. R., Carrillo, J. E., & Ananeh-Firempong, O. II. (2003). Defining cultural competence: A practical framework for addressing racial/ethnic disparities in health and health care. *Public Health Reports*, 118(4), 293–302.

Blanchet Garneau, A., & Pepin, J. (2015). Cultural competence: A constructivist definition. *Journal of Transcultural Nursing*, 26(1), 9–15. https://doi.org/10.1177/104365961454129

Bloomberg, P., & Pitchford, B. (2023). *Leading impact teams: Building a culture of efficacy and agency*. Mimi & Todd Press.

Bonilla, S., Dee, T. S., & Penner, E. K. (2021). Ethnic studies increases longer-run academic engagement and attainment. *Proceedings of the National Academy of Sciences, Proceedings of the National Academy of Sciences*, 118(37), 2026386118.

Bowen, D. H., & Kisida, B. (2019). *Investigating causal effects of arts education experiences: Experimental evidence from Houston's Arts Access Initiative*. Houston Education Research Consortium.

Brown, T. (2009). *Change by Design: How Design Thinking Transforms Organizations and Inspires Innovation*. Harper

Brown, B. L. (2018). *Dare to lead: Brave work, tough conversations, whole hearts*. Random House.

Cabrera, N. L., Milem, J. F., Jaquette, O., & Marx, R. W. (2014). *Missing the (Student Achievement) forest for all the (political) trees: Empiricism and the Mexican American Studies controversy in Tucson. American Educational Research Journal*, 51(6), 1084–1118.

Cardwell, M. E., Soliz, J., & Bergquist, G. L. (2020). Critical incidents in the development of (multi)ethnic-racial identity: Experiences of individuals with mixed ethnic-racial backgrounds in the U.S. *Journal of Social and Personal Relationships*, 37(5). https://doi.org/10.1177/0265407520906256

Carter, R. T. (1995). *The influence of race and racial identity in psychotherapy: Toward a racially inclusive model*. Wiley.

Christensen, L. (2000). *Reading, writing, and rising up: Teaching about social justice and the power of the written word*. Milwaukee, WI: Rethinking Schools.

Crenshaw, K. (1991). Mapping the margins: Intersectionality, identity politics, and violence against women of color. *Stanford Law Review*, 43(6), 1241–1299. https://doi.org/10.2307/1229039

Colwell, W., & Howard, B. (2018). *Youth equity stewardship: A student-led equity model for building cultures of belonging.* Thousand Oaks, CA: Corwin.

Confessore, N. (2023, December 10). As fury erupts over campus antisemitism, conservatives seize their moment. *New York Times.* https://www.nytimes.com/2023/12/10/us/universities-antisemitism-conservatives-liberals.html

Cormier, D. R. (2020). Assessing preservice teachers' cultural competence with the cultural proficiency continuum Q-sort. *Educational Researcher*, 50(1), 17–31. https://doi.org/10.3102/0013189X20936670

Corwin Press. (2020). *The impact of arts integration and creative expression on academic growth: Case study findings.* https://www.corwin.com/deepequity

Delpit, L. (2006). *Other people's children: Cultural conflict in the classroom* (2nd ed.). The New Press.

Dee, T. S., & Penner, E. K. (2016). The causal effects of cultural relevance: Evidence from an ethnic studies curriculum. *American Educational Research Journal*, 54(1). https://doi.org/10.3102/0002831216677002

Emdin, C. (2017). *For White folks who teach in the hood . . . and the rest of y'all too.* Beacon Press.

Farrington, C. A., Maurer, J., McBride, M., Nagaoka, J., Puller, J. S., Shewfelt, S., & Weiss, E. (2019). *Arts education and social-emotional learning outcomes: State of the field report.* University of Chicago Consortium on School Research and Ingenuity.

Freire, P. (2000). *Pedagogy of the oppressed* (30th anniversary ed.). Continuum International Publishing Group.

Fullan, M. (2016). *The new meaning of educational change* (5th ed.). Teachers.

Gabriel, R., & Allington, R. (2012). The MET project: The wrong $45 million question. *Educational Leadership*, 70(3), 44–49.

Gay, G. (2018). *Culturally responsive teaching: Theory, research, and practice* (3rd ed.). New York: Teachers College Press.

Ginwright, S., & Seigel, S. (2019, May 15). Social innovation alone can't solve racial inequity. *Stanford Social Innovation Review.* https://ssir.org/articles/entry/social_innovation_alone_cant_solve_racial_inequity

González, N., Moll, L., & Amanti C., eds. (2005). *Funds of knowledge: Theorizing practices in households, communities, and classrooms.* Lawrence Erlbaum.

Gooden, M. A., & Dantley, M. (2012). Centering race in a framework for leadership preparation. *Journal of Research on Leadership Education*, 7(2), 237-253.

Gorski, P. C. (2017). *Reaching and teaching students in poverty: Strategies for erasing the opportunity gap.* Teachers College Press.

Gorski, P. C., & Zenkov, K., eds. (2014). *The big lies of school reform: Finding better solutions for the future of public education.* Routledge.

Hall, E. T. (1976). *Beyond culture.* Anchor.

References

Hammond, Z. L. (2014). *Culturally responsive teaching and the brain: Promoting authentic engagement and rigor among culturally and linguistically diverse students.* Corwin.

Hammond, Z. (2015). *Culturally responsive teaching and the brain: Promoting authentic engagement and rigor among culturally and linguistically diverse students.* Corwin.

Hattie, J. (2012). *Visible learning for teachers: Maximizing impact on learning.* Routledge.

Hays, P. A. (2008). *Addressing cultural complexities in practice: Assessment, diagnosis, and therapy* (2nd ed.). American Psychological Association.

Hays, P. A. (2022). *Addressing cultural complexities in counseling and clinical practice: An intersectional approach* (4th ed.). American Psychological Association.

Helms, J. E. (1990). *Black and white racial identity: Theory, research and practice.* Greenwood Press.

Helms, J. E. (1994). Racial identity and career assessment. *Journal of Career Assessment,* 2(3).

Hidalgo, N. (1993). Multicultural teacher introspection. In T. Perry & J. Fraser (eds.), *Freedom's plow: Teaching in the multicultural classroom* (pp. 99–106). Routledge.

hooks, b. (1994). Teaching to transgress: Education as the practice of freedom. Routledge.

Howard, G. R. (2015). *We can't lead where we won't go: An educator's guide to equity.* Corwin Press.

Howard, G. R. (2016). *We can't teach what we don't know: White teachers, multiracial schools* (3rd ed.). Teachers College Press.

Howard, T. C., & Rodriguez, L. F. (2000). Creating culturally responsive pedagogy for African American and Latino students. *The High School Journal,* 83(2), 1-11.

Ishimaru, A. M. (2020). *Just schools: Building equitable collaborations with families and communities.* Teachers College Press.

Jordan, C. H., Amir, D., & Bloom, P. (2019). Lacking a clear and stable sense of self undermines empathy. *Emotion,* 19(6), 1097–1106.

Khalifa, M. A., Gooden, M. A., & Davis, J. E. (2016). Culturally responsive school leadership: A synthesis of the literature. *Review of Educational Research,* 86(4), 1272-1311.

Ladson-Billings, G. (1994). *The dreamkeepers: Successful teachers of African American children.* Jossey-Bass.

Ladson-Billings, G. (1995). Toward a theory of culturally relevant pedagogy. *American Educational Research Journal,* 32(3), 465–491.

Ladson-Billings, G. (2009). *The dreamkeepers: Successful teachers of African American children* (2nd ed.). Jossey-Bass.

Lekoko, R. N. (2007). Story-telling as a potent research paradigm for indigenous communities. *AlterNative: An International Journal of Indigenous Peoples,* 3(2). https://doi.org/10.1177/117718010700300206

Love, B. L. (2019). *We want to do more than survive: Abolitionist teaching and the pursuit of educational freedom.* Beacon Press.

Love, B. L. (2023). *Punished for dreaming: How school reform harms black children and how we heal.* New York: St. Martin's Press.

Lyons, O., & Moyers, B. (1991, July 3). *Oren Lyons the Faithkeeper with Bill Moyers* [Interview transcript]. PBS. https://www-tc.pbs.org/moyers/faithandreason/print/pdfs/faithkeeper.pdf

Milner, H. R. IV. (2020). *Start where you are* (2nd ed.). Teachers College Press.

Milner, H. R. (2020). *Start where you are, but don't stay there: Understanding diversity, opportunity gaps, and teaching in today's classrooms* (2nd ed.). Harvard Education Press.

National Equity Project. (n.d.). *Liberatory design.* Retrieved February 24, 2025, from https://www.nationalequityproject.org/frameworks/liberatory-design

New England College Personnel Association. (n.d.). Land acknowledgement. ACPA – College Student Educators International. Retrieved January 7, 2025, from https://newengland.myacpa.org/about/land-acknowledgement/

Palmer, P. J. (2017). *The courage to teach: Exploring the inner landscape of a teacher's life* (20th anniversary ed.). Jossey-Bass.

Paris, D., & Alim, H. S. (2017). *Culturally sustaining pedagogies: Teaching and learning for justice in a changing world.* Teachers College Press.

Park, D. C., & Huang, C.-M. (2010). Culture wires the brain: A cognitive neuroscience perspective. Perspectives on Psychological Science, 5(4). https://doi.org/10.1177/1745691610374591

Pennington, C. R., Heim, D., Levy, A. R., & Larkin, D. T. (2016). Twenty years of stereotype threat research: A review of psychological mediators. *PLOS One.* https://doi.org/10.1371/journal.pone.0146487.

Ravitch, D. (2013). *Reign of error: The hoax of the privatization movement and the danger to America's public schools.* Vintage Press.

Renken, E. (2020, April 11). How stories connect and persuade us: Unleashing the brain power of narrative. *NPR.* https://www.npr.org/sections/health-shots/2020/04/11/815573198/how-stories-connect-and-persuade-us-unleashing-the-brain-power-of-narrative

Rezvani, S., & Gordon, S. A. (2021, November 1). How sharing our stories builds inclusion. *Harvard Business Review.* https://hbr.org/2021/11/how-sharing-our-stories-builds-inclusion.

Roorda, D. L., Koomen, H. M. Y., Spilt, J. L., & Oort, F. J. (2011). The influence of affective teacher-student relationships on students' school engagement and achievement: A meta-analytic approach. *Review of Educational Research*, 81(4), 493–529.

Roschuni, C. N., Goodman, E., & Agogino, A. M. (2013). *Communicating actionable user research for human-centered design. AI EDAM*, 27(2), 143–154. https://doi.org/10.1017/S0890060413000048

Safir, S., & Dugan, J. (2021). *Street data.* Corwin.

Schniedewind, N., & Sapon-Shevin, M. (2012). *Educational courage: Resisting the ambush of public education.* Beacon Press.

References

Shade, B. J. R., Kelly, C., & Oberg, M. (1997). *Creating culturally responsive classrooms*. American Psychological Association.

Singleton, G. E. (2021). *Courageous conversations about race: A field guide for achieving equity in schools* (3rd ed.). Corwin Press.

Sleeter, C. E. (2003). Critical multiculturalism and globalization: A pedagogy of connection. In G. E. Fishman & P. McLaren (eds.), *Rethinking multicultural education for the next generation: Critical multiculturalism and globalization* (pp. 147–159). Routledge.

Steele, C. M., & Aronson, J. (2005). Stereotype threat. In J. F. Dovidio, P. Glick, & L. A. Rudman (Eds.), *On the nature of prejudice: Fifty years after Allport* (pp. 369–386). Blackwell.

Suzuki, W. A., Feliú-Mójer, M. I., Hasson, U., Yehuda, R., & Zarate, J. M. (2018). Dialogues: The science and power of storytelling. *Journal of Neuroscience*, 38(44), 9468–9470. https://doi.org/10.1523/JNEUROSCI.1942-18.2018

Tatum, B. D. (1992). Talking about race, learning about racism: The application of racial identity development theory in the classroom. *Harvard Educational Review*, 62(1), 1–24.

Tucker-Ray, W., Anaissie, T., Cary, V., Clifford, D., Malarkey, T., Wise, S., & the National Equity Project and Stanford d.school K12 Lab. (2016). *Liberatory Design: A Framework*. National Equity Project & Stanford d.school.

Utt, J., & Tochluk, S. (2020). White teacher, know thyself: Improving anti-racist praxis through racial identity development. *Urban Education,* 55(1), 125–152. https://doi.org/10.1177/0042085916648741

Villegas, A. M., & Lucas, T. (2002). *Educating culturally responsive teachers: A coherent approach*. SUNY Press.

Warren, M. R., Hong, S., Rubin, C. L., & Uy, P. S. (2009). Beyond the bake sale: A community-based relational approach to parent engagement in schools. *Teachers College Record*, 111(9), 2209-2254.

Walton, G. M., & Spencer, S. J. (2009). Latent ability: Grades and test scores systematically underestimate the intellectual ability of negatively stereotyped students. *Psychological Science*, 20(9). https://doi.org/10.1111/j.1467-9280.2009.02417

Weinstein, C. S., Tomlinson-Clarke, S., & Curran, M. (2004). Toward a conception of culturally responsive classroom management. *Journal of Teacher Education*, 55(1), 25-38.

Welton, A. D., Mansfield, K. C., Lee, P. L., & Young, M. D. (2018). Hiring culturally responsive school leaders: A principal pipeline problem. *Educational Administration Quarterly*, 54(4), 609-644.

Wexler, B. E. (2006). *Brain and culture: Neurobiology, ideology, and social change*. MIT Press.

Wiggins, G. (2012). Seven keys to effective feedback. *Educational Leadership*, 70(1). Association for Supervision and Curriculum Development (ASCD).

Wijaya Mulya, T., Aditomo, A., & Suryani, A. (2022). On being a religiously tolerant Muslim: Discursive contestations among pre-service teachers in contemporary Indonesia. *British Journal of Religious Education*, 44(1), 66–79. https://doi.org/10.1080/01416200.2021.1917338

Index

Achievement Triangle, 12–13, 39–41

Action
- stewardship as action rooted in knowledge and care, 5, 72–74
- creative resistance as action, 187–199

Action research, 179–182

Agency, 2–6, 170–172, 213–218
- creative resistance and, 187–208
- student voice and, 170–172, 213–218
- see also Student voice

Affirmation Before Reformation, 8–9

Assessment
- climate assessment, 44–46
- school outcomes assessment, 47–49
- privilege and power assessment, 133–136
- Seven Commitments assessment, 165–167
- see also Four A's

Banks, James, 79–85

Belonging, 1–6, 79–85, 145–153

Bloomberg, Paul J., 20–24

Catalysts for Growth, 54–56

Climate Assessment, 44–46

Collaborative inquiry, 19–24
- in practice, 24–29
- and Streams of Engagement, 30–32
- see also Impact Teams

Collective efficacy, 20–24

Community
- Story, Trust, & Community Journey (Stream 2), 64–67
- Intergenerational Partnership & Practice (Stream 4), 145–149
- see also belonging; trust

Culture, 79–85
- cultural competence, 85–90, 105–110
- identity triangle, 94–97
- lenses of difference, 91–94
- stereotype threat research, 102–104

Culture Toss, 98–101

Democracy, 1–6, 187–191

Desert Monsoon Model, 213–217
- Five Aspects of, 218–222
- see also Agency; Student voice

Dialogue, 68–71
- see also Homelands Conversation; collaborative inquiry

Dominance to Justice Word Association, 128–130

Dynamics of Social Dominance, 131–133

Emdin, Christopher, 6

Empowered Stewardship Outcomes, 9–11

Engagement Strategies
- Stream 1 overview, 36–37
- Stream 2 overview, 65–67
- Stream 3 overview, 122–124
- Stream 4 overview, 148–149

Equity, 1–6, 120–144
- systemic inequity, 120–137
- see also Justice; Power

Evidence
- in collaborative inquiry, 19–29
- in Seven Commitments assessment, 165–167

Index

Feedback
    Glow and Grow, 170–172
    Kudos and Challenges, 57–59
    see also assessment

Formative assessment
    see Assessment; Four A's; Glow and Grow

Four A's, 18–22, 60–62

Gay, Geneva, 6

Glow and Grow, 170–172

Hammond, Zaretta, 6, 105–110

Healing, 5–6, 187–212

Homelands Conversation, 68–71

Howard, Gary, 4–6

House of Learning
    invitation into, 151–155

Identity Triangle, 94–97

Impact
    Seven Commitments action research project, 179–182

Impact Teams, 20–24

In Lak'ech, 75–78

In My One Beat, 115–119

In My One Beat – Struggle, 142–144

Intergenerational learning
    Intergenerational Partnership & Practice (Stream 4), 145–153

Intergenerational Partnership & Practice (Stream 4), 145–183

Justice, 120–144
    Justice in the Words of Elders, 137–141
    see also Equity; Power

Kudos and Challenges, 57–59

Ladson-Billings, Gloria, 79–85

Layers of Engagement, 15–17

Leadership, 15–17, 168–169
    see also Learning From and With Colleagues; Impact Teams

Learning From and With Colleagues, 168–169

Milner, H. Richard, 6

Nican Tlaca, 125–127

Personal Growth Project, 111–114

Power, 131–137
    privilege and power assessment, 133–136
    see also Equity; Justice

Privilege and Power Assessment, 133–136

Professional learning
    Learning From and With Colleagues, 168–169
    Seven Commitments study groups, 161–164

Questions to Consider, 42–43

Reflection, 42–43, 111–114, 165–167
    see also Personal Growth Project; Questions to Consider

Resistance, 187–199
    see also Creative Resistance (Stream 5); justice

Roots of Stewardship
    Part 1, 192–196
    Part 2, 197–198

Seven Commitments of Stewardship
    introduction, 14–17
    practice framework, 150–155
    application, 156–160
    study groups, 161–164
    assessment, 165–167
    action research project, 179–182
    student-centered project, 183–186

Shifting the Emotional Paradigm, 208–212

Social Dominance to Justice for All (Stream 3), 120–144

Stages of Organizational Growth, 50–53

Stages of Personal Growth Toward Cultural Competence, 105–110

Stewardship
- definition, 5, 72–74
- and democracy, 1–6
- and equity, 1–6
- see also Seven Commitments of Stewardship; Youth Empowered Stewardship

Streams of Engagement, 30–32
- Riverbed (Stream 1), 35–62
- Story, Trust, & Community Journey (Stream 2), 64–119
- Social Dominance to Justice for All (Stream 3), 120–144
- Intergenerational Partnership & Practice (Stream 4), 145–183
- Creative Resistance (Stream 5), 187–223

Stereotype Threat Research, 102–104

Story, Trust, & Community Journey (Stream 2), 64–119

Student voice, 170–172, 213–218
- see also Agency

Systems change
- systemic inequity, 120–137
- Stages of Organizational Growth, 50–53

Transformation, 1–6, 120–144, 187–212

Trust, 64–71
- see also Story, Trust, & Community Journey (Stream 2)

Voice
- student voice, 170–172, 213–218
- see also agency; Desert Monsoon Model

We, the People / Nican Tlaca, 125–127

Youth Empowered Stewardship (YES), 2–6
- collaborative inquiry process, 20–29
- Streams of Engagement, 30–32
- see also Stewardship

Thank you!

Mimi & Todd Press exclusively publishes authors who are dedicated to making an impact through their work. By purchasing, reading and implementing their ideas, you deepen the impact and increase awareness for future learning.

More from Mimi & Todd Press:

Leading Impact Teams: Building a Culture of Efficacy and Agency
Paul Bloomberg and Barb Pitchford

Re-Envisioning Rigor Books 1, 2 and 3
Michael McDowell and Aaron Eisberg

Belonging Through a Culture of Dignity: The Keys to Successful Equity Implementation
Floyd Cobb and John Krownapple

The Project Habit: Making Rigorous PBL Doable
Michael McDowell and Kelley S. Miller

Amplify Learner Voice through Culturally Responsive and Sustaining Assessment
Paul Bloomberg, Kara Vandas, Ingrid Twyman, et al.

Peer Power: Unite, Learn and Prosper: Activate an Assessment Revolution
Paul Bloomberg, Barb Pitchford, Kara Vandas, et al.

Arrows: A Systems-Based Approach to School Leadership
Carrie Rosebrock and Sarah Henry

Learner Agency: A Field Guide for Taking Flight
Kara Vandas, Jeanette Westfall, and Ashley Duvall

mimitoddpress.com

Mimi & Todd Press discovers and publishes purpose-driven thought leaders who are striving to make a difference in the world. Visit us online to browse our catalogue of books and learn more.

Competency Over Conformity

Embrace the power of personalized learning and unlock your potential with Competency-Based Learning.

Literacy and Justice for All

Discover the power of a comprehensive, research-based literacy education that meets the needs of every student.

Join Our Impact Team Community

Join our learner-centered PLC community where we put students in the driver's seat!

Let's create schools that work for all of us!

Build multigenerational partnerships with **YES!** (Youth Equity Stewardship).

www.ingramcontent.com/pod-product-compliance
Lightning Source LLC
Chambersburg PA
CBHW040008080526
44586CB00028B/2928